"While scientists struggle to understand the biological bases of autism to create preventions, treatments and cures, Dr. Firestone and her colleagues at The Help Group bring hope and help to families today. *Autism Heroes* sensitively tells the stories of courageous families that live with autism. It will bring guidance and support to other parents and inspiration to clinicians and scientists."

David G. Amaral, PhD, Professor, Department of Psychiatry and Behavioral Sciences, Director of Research, The M.I.N.D. Institute at the University of California, Davis

"I greatly admire Dr. Barbara Firestone's lifetime dedication, leadership and commitment to helping young people with special needs. She shares her experience and insight in this wonderful book in a way that not only raises awareness and understanding about autism but is profoundly impactful."

Representative Howard L. Berman, US Congress

"In *Autism Heroes*, Barbara Firestone shines a light on the heroic families who are building hopeful futures for their children, and Joe Buissink's images enable us to meet them firsthand. This invaluable book motivates us to vigorously continue our work on behalf of all families living with autism."

John L. Burton, President pro Tem of the California State Senate (Ret.), Founder, John Burton Foundation

"*Autism Heroes* is a gift to the autism community. Raising a child with autism has never been easy, but it just got easier, thanks to Barbara Firestone's wisdom and compassion, Joe Buissink's sensitive images, and the courageous families willing to share their most intimate stories with her. Pediatricians can now say to families coping with a new diagnosis, have I got a book for you!"

Eileen Costello, MD, Pediatrician, co-author of Quirky Kids: Understanding and Helping Your Child Who Doesn't Fit In

"In *Autism Heroes* Dr. Firestone's commentary and intimate conversations with parents facing the challenges of autism, and Joe Buissink's images, are insightful and deeply affecting. This hopeful book is a must read for families, teachers and clinicians. In its pages you will meet true heroes."

David T. Feinberg, MD, MBA, Professor of Clinical Psychiatry, David Geffen School of Medicine, University of California, Los Angeles, CEO, UCLA Hospital System

"*Autism Heroes* is a passionate and brilliant compilation of stories and photographs that portray both the challenges and joys of living with children who have autism. Dr. Firestone captures the enormity and range of experiences that parents face as well as the new frontiers of hope. Inspirational, provocative and painstakingly honest, *Autism Heroes* poignantly reminds us of the ongoing need to educate and advocate on behalf of children and families."

Areva D. Martin, Esq., Managing Partner, Martin & Martin, LLP, President, Special Needs Network, Inc., parent of a child with an autism spectrum disorder

"Few have the combination of compassion, rigorous knowledge, passion for the field, and accomplishments in helping literally thousands of children with autism spectrum disorders as does Barbara Firestone. She is also an extraordinary listener, and a great observer of people, making her perspectives and collection of family stories, coupled with Joe Buissink's photography, extremely rich, inspiring, and instructive."

Michael O'Hanlon, Senior Fellow, Brookings Institution, parent of child with an autism spectrum disorder

"I read Dr. Firestone's inspiring book with considerable awe and admiration. Autism touches the lives of millions of children and their families in ways both daunting and profound. The accumulated wisdom of the poignant personal experiences that are selflessly shared in this excellent book will help to dismantle the ignorance and misinformation that has typically stigmatized autism, and has made life more difficult for the children and families who live and cope with it. The private challenges, heartaches, and triumphs revealed by these families should raise public awareness, and promote advanced research, program development and expansion, so that effective changes for children with autism and their families can one day take place. The bravery, hope, and love contained within these pages are nothing short of transformational, and much can be learned from reading *Autism Heroes*."

Cheryl Saban, PhD, CEO, Saban Family Foundation, Founder of 50 Ways to Save our Children, 50ways.org

"*Autism Heroes* provides a timely and touching perspective into the personal struggles, challenges and resiliency of parents of children with autism spectrum disorders. Dr. Firestone's enlightening book is certain to be an important resource for other parents, educators and scientists trying to understand this baffling disorder."

Paul Satz, PhD, Professor of Medical Psychology/Neuropsychology, Emeritus, David Geffen School of Medicine at UCLA

"As a researcher who has spent over 30 years working with families of children with autism, I have been continually impressed with the courage, strength, dedication and sheer determination of these families. It is the parents who keep us professionals grounded in what is important. They point us in the right direction. After reading *Autism Heroes*, who could doubt it?"

Laura Schreibman, PhD, Distinguished Professor, Director, UCSD Autism Research Program, University of California, San Diego, author of The Science and Fiction of Autism

"*Autism Heroes* compels us to redouble our efforts to expand opportunities for children with autism and intensify our support for their courageous parents. As Vice Chair of the California Legislative Blue Ribbon Commission on Autism, Dr. Firestone brings the voices of families to the public policy arena to promote change and give meaning to hope."

Darrell Steinberg, California State Senator, Chair, California Legislative Blue Ribbon Commission on Autism

"As a parent of a child with autism I am forever grateful for the commitment, hope and expertise that Dr. Firestone brings into our lives. In *Autism Heroes*, Dr. Firestone, Joe Buissink and 38 families sensitively embrace other families coping with this experience. This remarkable book will surely strike a chord with all who read it."

Louis A. Vismara, MD, Consultant to Senator Don Perata, President pro Tem, California State Senate, Co-founder, The M.I.N.D. Institute at the University of California, Davis, Commissioner, First 5 California

"One of the parents in this moving and important book says 'more information equals less fear.' With this book, Dr. Firestone will help parents of children with autism replace those fears with hope. This book will be an invaluable resource to families who are confronting the challenges of autism."

Representative Henry A. Waxman, US Congress

"In our journey along life's pebbled path, it is through the personal stories of others that we bind the start to the finish. In *Autism Heroes*, we have the privilege of meeting families through their words and images who have found their way forward, despite extraordinary challenges. Dr. Firestone's book is truly illuminating and informative."

Peter C. Whybrow, MD, Director, Semel Institute for Neuroscience and Human Behavior at the University of California, Los Angeles

"Barbara Firestone's book is truly an inspiration that carries an important message of hope. *Autism Heroes* is an intimate portrait of 38 families and their celebration of love, commitment, and pride in their own words and through Joe Buissink's lens. A must read for families everywhere beginning their journey."

Nancy D. Wiseman, Founder and President, First Signs, author of Could It Be Autism? A Parent's Guide to the First Signs and Next Steps, *parent of child with an autism spectrum disorder*

autism
heroes

Barbara Firestone, PhD

autism
heroes

Portraits of Families Meeting the Challenge

Forewords by
Teddi and Gary Cole
and Catherine Lord, PhD

Photography by Joe Buissink

First published in 2008
by Jessica Kingsley Publishers
116 Pentonville Road
London N1 9JB, UK
and
400 Market Street, Suite 400
Philadelphia, PA 19106, USA

www.jkp.com

Library of Congress Cataloging in Publication Data
A CIP catalog record for this book is available from the
Library of Congress

British Library Cataloguing in Publication Data
A CIP catalogue record for this book is available from the British
Library

ISBN 978 1 84310 837 5

Printed and bound in the People's Republic of China

For the many families who have confronted the challenges of autism. Their strength, love, wisdom and resilience are at the very heart of this book and lead the way for other families just beginning the journey.

In memory of my parents and grandparents who believed that the education of children is one of life's noblest callings.

Barbara Firestone

For my son, Benno, who has taught me so many things about life and how to live it.

Joe Buissink

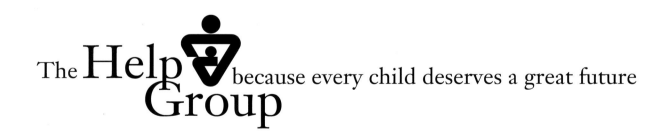

The Help Group
because every child deserves a great future

All book royalties are being donated to The Help Group in support of its efforts on behalf of children with autism spectrum disorders and their families.

contents

foreword by teddi and gary cole

It seems like an eternity since our daughter Mary was diagnosed with an autism spectrum disorder. When Dr. Barbara Firestone, one of our personal heroes, asked us if we would share the story of our journey, we agreed because we wanted other families to know that there is hope. In *Autism Heroes* she has brought together parents from all backgrounds with children with autism spectrum disorders who share their experiences of dignity, hope, opportunity and love.

All of the families who took part in this book, including us, have heard the words, "your child has autism," yet we have never given up on our children, no matter how daunting the diagnosis may have sounded, and no matter how little hope we may have been given at the time. Our journeys are filled with more emotional highs and lows than any parent of a typically developing child might ever expect to experience in a lifetime. It is quite difficult to explain to those who have not lived through the tears or the laughter, and the insights we have gained from our children. Although at times we have felt deep despair, we have witnessed mountains of hope. We have had the opportunity to meet some of the finest people in the world, from clinicians and teachers to parents of typical children who want to understand our children and support their victories.

The universe is as full of remarkable people and children as life is full of surprises. It is no surprise, however, that we all want the best for our children. We all want them to reach their fullest potential. The Help Group reminds us that "every child deserves a great future." As parents of children with autism spectrum disorders, we want you to know that we are here for your children and we are here for you.

Somewhere in this book, you may see a family like yours or a family like one you know. It is our hope that if you are a parent of a child with autism, or suspect that your child may have autism, you will derive strength from each of these families as you tackle the challenges, no matter how difficult the challenges may seem. *Autism Heroes* is about our families and our beautiful children from whom we have learned so much. They have taught us indescribable lessons of humanity, judgment, unconditional love and most of all, hope for the future. As parents, we would like to thank Dr. Firestone for having the insight and the vision to create *Autism Heroes* to support other families just beginning the journey, or already on the journey.

Teddi and Gary Cole
Actors, advocates and parents of a
child with an autism spectrum disorder

foreword by catherine lord, PhD

Many professionals who work with children and adolescents with autism spectrum disorders (ASDs), when asked why we do such work, will recount the charm, beauty, challenges and continuing wonder of our patients and clients with autism, young and old. Yet anyone who stays in this field for more than a few years knows that there are other heroes in this story: the parents who care and fight for their children with love, bravery and creativity.

In *Autism Heroes*, Dr. Barbara Firestone gives us a look through windows of different shapes and sizes and hues into how families with a child with autism think and live with grace and hope. Those of us who work with families and children but do not have children with autism ourselves will never really know how it feels to deal with the anger, the sadness, the exhaustion and the continual need to advocate and educate others. Through the compelling narrative we experience both universal themes and variations, showing that there is not only one way to do this and that there are common strategies and sources of support.

One of my favorite statements was made by Hilary and Bob Kip about taking their children into the community—to be willing to put yourself and your child out in the world, but first to be prepared, to pick your battles, quickly, and to never give up. It embodies all those steps that could form a "cheer" of support for families living with autism. One of our jobs as autism clinicians is to help in the preparation, decrease the battles and never give up the cheer.

There are many other words of wisdom in this wonderful book. The importance of having an educational program that parents trust and that values families. The need to seek and accept support from families, friends, professionals, and the autism community. The point, as several of the parents said, is to find strengths, in the children, in the parents, in the community, and to build on them.

For many families with children with ASDs, knowledge is an important strength—knowledge about their own child, about ASDs in general, about their community resources. Whenever our clinic gets new staff, they are always shocked at how much most of the parents know.

Yet we are all at some point humbled by how little we know about the development of this complex disorder or disorders that are called ASDs, and what is best for each child. Ultimately, families have jobs on multiple levels, from advocate and chauffeur to cheerleader and tutor. I was struck by another statement in the book, that families need to let their children see them enjoying life—because life is more than Individual Education Plans and therapy sessions and passing tests and reaching milestones. This seems like an extremely important point to consider, not just for the immediate family of a child with ASD, but also for extended families trying to support their children and brothers and sisters who are parents of children with autism.

This book inspired me to think harder and more carefully about the families with whom I work and the nature of their job, and my job in supporting them. In the rich landscape that Dr. Firestone has created in *Autism Heroes*, the families speak for themselves with spirit and dignity, and we can all gain much from listening to them.

Catherine Lord, PhD
Director, University of Michigan Autism and Communication Disorders Center
Professor of Psychology and Psychiatry
Research Professor, Center for Human Growth and Development

preface

I vividly remember the day when one little boy would introduce me to autism and inspire my life's work.

When I was a freshman in college I participated in a field trip to a state institution for individuals with severe disabilities as part of a required speech/communications class. At first, we had no idea what this had to do with our course. Each of us was assigned to spend an hour with one of the resident children. After a few minutes with Timmy, I was struck by the fact that although he was nine years old, he could not speak, he made no eye contact, and he rocked back and forth. He appeared to be locked inside a world of his own. I used all of my youthful energy and enthusiasm to repeatedly try to engage him, but I could not make contact with him. I sang, I made funny faces and noises, jumped up and down, and exhausted just about everything in my bag of tricks. I was totally unsuccessful, dismayed and confused.

I was told by a staff member on the unit that Timmy had a condition called autism—I had never met anyone with this disorder and had never heard of it. In addition to the behaviors I observed, I was told that Timmy had no self care skills, had severe behavioral issues and was, at times, self-injurious. I could not believe the plight of this child and thought about what life must be like for him. I asked about his family and was told that due to the scarcity of resources in the community, his parents had no choice but to place him in this institution where he could be safe and his basic needs could be met.

On our return back to campus, our professor, Dr. Mary Ann Peins, explained why she took us on this field trip. She spoke about the nature and power of human communication and its role in connecting us to others. She spoke about the profound impact that the lack of communicative ability can have as it did on the children whom we met that day. I asked her what type of professionals worked with these children. She mentioned that speech pathologists had a very important role to play and that she was a speech pathologist. I asked if my college offered a major in this area and she said, "Yes."

I could not set aside my thoughts of Timmy and his family, or the intensity of my desire to know more about autism. My next step seemed clear to me. When I returned to my dorm, I called my parents to tell them that I now knew what I wanted to study and what I wanted to do with my future. This experience with one little boy prompted the course of my studies and my lifelong commitment to helping children with special needs and their families.

Four decades have passed since my visit to the state institution during a time that we now look upon as the dark ages of autism. It was a period characterized by stigma, misconceptions and lack of opportunity. Since those days, parents and professionals have worked incredibly hard on behalf of children with autism. Due to their efforts and the ever increasing number of children affected, the race has accelerated to find the causes and the interventions that hold promise, and to ensure that children with autism are given the opportunity to fully realize their potential. It is a race that can never be fast enough for the parents who are engaged in their own marathon to find the information and resources that can make the critical difference for their children.

acknowledgements

Autism Heroes was born of the dedication and passion of a wonderful group of individuals.

I'd like to express my heartfelt appreciation to the 38 families who opened their hearts and shared their stories with me and gave me the privilege of illuminating my book with their insight and wisdom, and especially to the children who have inspired the labor of love that is *Autism Heroes*.

I am forever grateful to my husband, David, who possesses a great sensitivity and understanding of children with special needs. He has wholeheartedly supported my life's work from the very beginning. Over a decade ago, David penned a phrase that means a great deal to The Help Group and to me—"Dignity, hope, opportunity and love are the birthrights of all children." This quotation speaks to core beliefs of The Help Group and forms the framework of my book. David has contributed greatly to this book and has encouraged me every step of the way.

Joe Buissink has generously given of his time and enormous talent to capturing the beautiful images of the families portrayed in this book. His involvement as an artist and as the parent of a child with an autism spectrum disorder is very special.

I thank Dr. Catherine Lord and Teddi and Gary Cole for gracing my book with their forewords. Dr. Lord's work in the field has been extraordinary and has created a beacon of hope for children and families. The Coles have dedicated themselves to helping their daughter Mary to blossom and advocate to building brighter futures for all children with autism spectrum disorders.

The Help Group is blessed with a remarkable Board of Directors who dedicates its efforts to opening the doors of opportunity to children with special needs. My thanks to Gary H. Carmona, Susan Berk, Robert Dorman, Dr. David Firestone, Perry Katz, Dr. Martin Lasky, Jerrold Monkarsh, Joy Monkarsh, Barry N. Nagoshiner, Judd Swarzman, Howard Tenenbaum and Richard M. Zelle for their unwavering commitment to our mission throughout the years and for their support of this project. Dr. Susan Berman and the executive team of The Help Group, administration and staff, governmental partners, philanthropic friends, and volunteers have enabled many thousands of children with special needs to realize their fullest potential. The Help Group is a wonderful family.

I'd like to recognize and thank all who have shared in my vision for this book and have worked with me to bring it to fruition, particularly Jessica Kingsley, Terry Marks, Cheryl Raver, Gerry Rosenblatt, Dr. Laurie Stephens, and Bob Rooney. I'd also like to thank Pam Clark, Dr. Mary Bauman, Nata Preis, Barry Berk, Marilyn Buissink, Tish O'Connor, Dana Levy, Lisa Manafian, Kristine Datastanyan, Anke Ueberberg, Tony Schiavo, Cindy Bassman and Greg Allen.

I have a great family who encouraged me to pursue this project—Sarah and Jeremy Milken, Samantha and Jonathan Firestone, and Shari Firestone. And my grandchildren, Jake, Marin, and Charlotte, too.

I am very grateful to my mentors who have meant so much to me—Dr. Paul Satz, Nolan Spencer, and Dr. Gerry Hasterok.

I deeply value the input and efforts of my colleagues and friends—Senator John Burton, Dr. Lou Vismara, Dick Costello, Eleni Tsakopoulos-Kounalakis, Arnie Kleiner, Bruce Berman, Dawn Taubin and Kevin McCormick.

Many thanks to you all!

introduction

The commitment and caring of the parents whom I have met are extraordinary—I am in awe of their ability to persevere and to do whatever it takes for the sake of their children and to endure and overcome the challenges. Although each family is unique, they are part of a greater family of parents who are engaged in the journey through the maze to a place of hope.

When parents have the first suspicion that their child may be developing differently, it can be a time of fear, denial and a time when information and support can be the lifeline that they need to help them through. It is a very personal journey that changes their lives forever. When asked what would have made this time in their lives more tenable, they said knowing that they were not alone, having the benefit of the advice, support and encouragement of other families who have weathered a similar storm, having access to up-to-date information and resources, and living in a community that understands and cares.

I wanted to reach out to parents in the privacy of their homes in as non-threatening and intimate of a context as possible and provide them with the support and wisdom of other parents. I asked parents who had children, preschoolers through young adults, with all forms and degrees of autism if they would be willing to share their very personal stories in words and images. The parents I asked are from all walks of life and are culturally diverse—some are single parents and others married. The response was overwhelmingly positive. They enthusiastically agreed to be interviewed, to have their interviews videotaped, transcribed and excerpted, as well as to have photographs taken of themselves and their children so that I could create a tapestry of their experiences.

They said that they understood how important their experiences could be to other parents—realizing in hindsight how impactful it might have been for them at the outset of their journeys. They said that they felt comfortable with full disclosure in the spirit of lifting the stigma. Although some were parents of children with classic autism and others were parents of children with high functioning autism or Asperger's Disorder or other variations of autism, there were many universal chords filled with a great deal of wisdom and a trajectory of hope.

As I sat across from these parents, they shared their very personal experiences. They spoke with openness, vulnerability and intimacy. At times, they fought back the tears in recounting the trials and in recounting the triumphs. And as I listened and guided them through the interview, I too held back the tears. I was overcome by the trust that the parents placed in me to convey their innermost thoughts and feelings to other parents and to the public.

I asked a highly acclaimed photographer, Joe Buissink, who has a child with an autism spectrum disorder, if he would be willing to shoot the photographs for this project. Without hesitation, he said that it would be his privilege to participate and offer his services on a pro bono basis—an incredible act of generosity and caring. Joe said that he knew firsthand what it means to be a parent in this situation and would do anything in his power to help other parents. When he looks through his camera to capture the beauty and essence of these parents and their children, his eyes, heart, and soul see the families with a crystal clear prism of love and understanding. Joe's photos reveal a great deal about each of the families and bring their words to life.

I am grateful to Jessica Kingsley for her confidence and support of this project.

When I approached Jessica and her organization to publish this book, they immediately agreed to carry this message of hope to families everywhere. With their vast experience in the publication of books on autism, they said that they knew how important the message of this book could be for parents of children with autism.

Everyone involved—the parents, Joe, my husband David and I, the publishing team and the project staff—were dedicated to the effort; it was a labor of love that took on a special life of its own.

Each of the parents whom I interviewed are heroes—heroic in their never ending efforts on behalf of their children and heroic in their willingness to lend their support to others just setting out on the journey. It became clear to me that this book should be named in their honor: *Autism Heroes: Portraits of Families Meeting the Challenge*. With candor and courage, they chart a course through the many stages of coping with autism and of overcoming the obstacles. It is a roadmap for other parents and a celebration of their commitment.

An ever increasing number of children are being diagnosed with autism spectrum disorders (ASDs)—now referred to by many as an epidemic. Once scarcely discussed in the media, autism now attracts a great deal of attention. The autism landscape is dramatically changing and the quest for answers intensifies.

In the 1960s and 70s, autism was considered a rare disorder and was estimated to affect four or five children per 10,000. These numbers stand in sharp contrast to the Centers for Disease Control and Prevention (CDC) that recently released a report estimating that one in every 150 children in the US has an autism spectrum disorder—a tenfold increase over the past decade. It occurs more frequently than childhood cancer, diabetes, and pediatric AIDS combined. Prevalence estimates are similar in other countries throughout the world who track this type of data.

Autism imposes many formidable challenges for each child and family whose lives it touches. It is a lifelong disability whose causes are yet to be identified. Autism spectrum disorders are characterized by a triad of challenges: communication impairments; problems with social interactions; and unusual, rigid and repetitive behaviors. The three most common disorders on the spectrum include autism, Asperger's Disorder and PDD-NOS (Pervasive Developmental Disorder—Not Otherwise Specified). ASDs range from mild to severe; no two children display the exact same characteristics. Some children develop atypically from birth, while a smaller percentage appear to develop normally and then begin to regress as toddlers. ASDs are four times more common in boys than in girls and impact children from all ethnic, cultural and socio-economic backgrounds.

Children with ASDs experience a complex set of challenges that is difficult to capture in a few paragraphs. Not intended to be a comprehensive list, here are some of the major characteristics often associated with classic autism and Asperger's Disorder.

Children with classic autism have severe impairments in language. Fifty percent are non verbal and 25 to 50 percent are thought to have mental retardation. With limited social interaction and eye contact, children with classic autism appear to be detached, lack interest in others and do not share their interests with others. Their play skills can be delayed, unusual, noninteractive and unimaginative. They can engage in stereotyped, repetitive, self stimulatory behaviors, and some children are self-injurious They have a need for sameness in their environment and have atypical reactions to sensory input like bright lights and loud noises. Their problems in language, social skills, and need for routine and sensory issues trigger tantrums and other behavior problems. For the diagnosis to be made, symptoms must be present before the age of three. The term high functioning autism, although not officially recognized as a diagnostic category, is commonly used to refer to children with autism whose intellectual capabilities are within the average to superior ranges and appear to have a greater degree of relatedness and less deviant language.

Children with Asperger's Disorder have serious challenges related to social interaction and understanding as well as to restricted and repetitive patterns of thought and behaviors. Unlike children with classic autism, children with Asperger's Disorder have average to superior intellectual capabilities, no significant clinical delays in language development and may have precocious language development.

Symptoms include preoccupation with a narrow range of subjects, an unusual, pedantic and monotonous speaking style that lacks prosody, and an inability to interpret the subtleties and nuances of language. Children with Asperger's Disorder have difficulties interpreting and responding to nonverbal cues, engaging in reciprocal two-way conversations, sharing interests with others, regulating emotions, managing anger, an inappropriate adherence to routines and rituals and immature empathy. Although they generally want to fit in, they face challenges forming peer friendships and are more comfortable with adults or younger children. In school settings they are often bullied, teased and ostracized by peers. Nearly two-thirds of adolescents experience affective disorders including anxiety disorders and depression. Problems with organizational skills such as completing a task, motor coordination, sensory input, over focus on parts of objects rather than the whole, and stereotyped or repetitive motor movements can also be present.

Although symptoms of Asperger's Disorder are present by the age of two or three, they are usually masked until after the age of five. Some do not consider Asperger's as part of the spectrum; others consider it a milder form of autism. Some adults with Asperger's make the case that it is a difference rather than a disorder.

The term PDD-NOS is used when a child's symptoms do not meet all of the criteria necessary for the diagnosis of any other autism spectrum disorder or other disorders that account for their symptoms.

The documented history of autism begins in 1943, when an Austrian child psychiatrist, Dr. Leo Kanner at Johns Hopkins University, first used the term autism to describe eleven children whose behaviors were consistent with what we define as classical autism. The term autism was derived from the Greek word *autos* that means "self." In 1911, Dr. Eugen Bleuler first used this term to describe adults with schizophrenia who seemed socially withdrawn. In 1944, Dr. Hans Asperger, a pediatrician in Vienna, quite separately from Dr. Kanner and unknown to one another, described the unusual behaviors of four boys that would lay the foundation for what is now known as Asperger's Disorder or Asperger's Syndrome. This disorder would not be officially recognized for 50 years. In 1994, Asperger's Syndrome was added to the *Diagnostic and Statistical Manual of Mental Disorders*, published by the American Psychiatric Association. Now in its fourth edition, this manual serves as the guide for diagnosis and clinical description of disorders and is widely used by professionals in the field.

In 1970, British psychiatrist and parent of a child with autism, Dr. Lorna Wing, and her colleague Dr. Judith Gould developed the concept of *autism spectrum disorders*. They characterized autism as a range of disorders based on difficulties with social interaction, communication and imagination. It encompasses children whose symptoms vary in type and intensity. In 1981, Dr. Wing first used the term Asperger's Syndrome to refer to children who were similar to those that Dr. Asperger originally described.

For many years autism was believed to have a psychological basis related to the mother's inability to bond with her child, the "Refrigerator Mom" theory. Although this theory, popularized by Bruno Bettelheim, has been discredited and set aside for more than 30 years, remnants of it still exist today. This interpretation coupled with the practice of institutionalizing children with classic autism gave rise to the stigma that was pervasive and painful to parents and children.

In the mid-1960s, a scientifically driven agenda for the research into the causes of autism began to emerge. Dr. Bernard Rimland, a researcher and parent of a child with autism, wrote a book that introduced the concept that autism had a neurobiological basis rather than being a result of poor parenting. The era of scientific research was about to begin.

During the same time period, intervention strategies began to be developed that were targeted at helping children to build essential skills. Dr. Ivar Lovaas at UCLA would introduce the behavioral treatment of autism. ABA (applied behavioral analysis) would set the stage for the development of evidence-based interventions, and remains the cornerstone of treatment for children with autism today.

Public policy reform began to emerge that would promote greater educational opportunity. For example in the United States, the *Education for All Handicapped Children Act* was passed in 1975 and renamed the *Individuals with Disabilities Education Act* in 1990. This landmark legislation mandated a free, appropriate, publicly supported education for all children with special needs in the least restrictive environment.

Over the past two decades, the number of children diagnosed with autism has continued to rise. The debate is robust. Some argue that this increase is due to improved diagnostic skills, decrease in misclassification, the broadening of diagnostic criteria, better documentation of identified cases, and overuse of the diagnosis or a combination of factors. Others argue that it is an absolute increase unexplained by these theories.

In its ongoing exploration of the causes of autism, scientific research is investigating the role of genetics and related heritability, vulnerability and susceptibility issues, and the potential role of other factors such as immune dysfunction, metabolic disturbances, infectious processes and environmental triggers. Research is beginning to more rigorously look at the questions of effective diagnostic, education and treatment models.

As public awareness continues to grow, the importance of early detection and early intervention is gaining greater attention. Research supports that classic autism can be reliably detected as early as 18 months in many cases, and that some symptoms appear during the first year of life. Intensive early intervention can enable children to make significant gains due to the neuroplasticity of the developing brain.

However, most children with ASDs are diagnosed at four years of age or later. Reportedly, factors related to socio-economic disadvantage, lack of access, and ethnicity may contribute to greater than average delays. A relatively small percentage of children who are diagnosed early receive the intensive intervention that they need. Services are either inadequate in the hours of therapy provided, unavailable, unaffordable, not publicly funded, or not covered by insurance companies in many communities. This is an important example of research advancing our understanding and the development of interventions, but the resources available to meet this demand lagging far behind.

It is therefore critical for parents to know that there are interventions that can make an important difference for their children and to advocate for these services for their children. Children with all types of ASDs can develop skills that enable them to lead more positive and productive lives. There is no single approach that addresses the needs of all children—there is no panacea, but there is hope.

The number of interventions available has continued to expand—some have the benefit of scientific study and varying degrees of validation. Others do not have the validation of science to support them but are anecdotally reported to be beneficial to some children based on the experience and data collected by educators and clinicians. It can be very confusing and parents must be careful not to forego established treatments to pursue unproven or potentially harmful treatments. Pharmacological approaches should be used judiciously and very carefully monitored. A full range of programs are not available in all communities, but parents must be encouraged to explore all of the available options.

Comprehensive programs capitalize on the child's relative strengths and interests, are highly structured and incorporate behavioral, developmental approaches comprising evidence-based best practices. These approaches recognize the complexities and variations of each child. Education and treatment promote growth in communication, social, behavioral, cognitive, academic and self help skills, and, motor development.

Programs for children with ASDs should be based on each child's unique needs. The most appropriate program may be school based in special education or regular education settings and/or after-school, clinic, or in-home based. With a highly structured educational and skill development approach, program components can include applied behavioral analysis, speech and language therapy, occupational therapy, social skills and adaptive living skills, training and adaptive physical education. Positive behavioral supports based on functional analysis of problem behavior should be part of the program. Progress must be tracked and reviewed in all areas on an ongoing basis.

Children ages three through five years with classic autism and high functioning autism can benefit from intensive specialized interdisciplinary preschool programs that provide a minimum of 25 hours per week of instruction with supportive services incorporated into the school day. There is a high staff to student ratio (at least one-to-three) including one-to-one and small group instruction. Preschool programs that emphasize strong collaboration among the professional and paraprofessional staff, and parents as key members of the team, significantly improve children's ability to acquire, retain, and generalize skills. In addition to one-to-one instruction and behavioral therapy these programs can include naturalistic approaches, specialized preschools, focus on structured early play activities, language and social skills development, and learning-readiness skills. For children younger than three who have been identified with ASDs, early intervention can include parent training and support, behavioral, speech, and occupational therapy, and strategies to encourage social play.

In addition to the general components of effective autism programs, children with classic autism can benefit from functional academics, augmentative communication approaches, daily-living skills instruction, and job-readiness training. Functional academics help students develop basic math and reading skills that are necessary for living more independently, for example, making change, reading street signs, and telling time. Daily-living skills and job-readiness training that focus on such skills as cooking, cleaning, shopping, using public transportation, and sorting items prepare students to be more

productive as adults. When ready, students can be placed in supervised work experiences in the community. An augmentative communication approach exposes students who are non-verbal, or who have limited verbal abilities, to a range of communication options that help the teacher/therapist identify the most useful method of communication. Alternative methods can include signing, use of pictures, computer-generated language and verbalizations that substitute for actual words. These programs demonstrate that children with more severe forms of autism can, and do, make strides in their development.

Children with Asperger's Disorder and high functioning autism require programs and services that directly teach social skills. Social skills training can be provided in regular education and special education settings, after-school groups, and in counseling and therapy programs. Social skills training helps children to develop the skills to interact more appropriately with others, to read facial expressions and body language, to take other people's thoughts and feelings into account, and to form friendships. Equipped with these skills, children are able to tear down the walls of isolation that surround them, reduce their anxiety and frustration, regulate their emotions and become more fully engaged in the world around them.

■ ■ ■

Important history is in the making for autism, as science, public policy, advocacy, best practices in education and treatment, and public awareness endeavors expand and intensify. Progress in these arenas will surely make the journey less arduous for children and families living with autism.

I invite you to meet 38 remarkable families who began their journeys at various times over the past two decades. With sensitivity and openness, they have shared their experiences so that other families may derive strength and support from their insights. They speak of the meaning of dignity, hope opportunity and love in their lives. It is a privilege to introduce these heroic parents to you.

dignity

- Cole ▪ Calzada ▪ Bradshaw
- Guruji ▪ Bentson-Geyer ▪ Peyser
- Rosen ▪ Gour ▪ del Olmo

When her son Nick was diagnosed with high functioning autism, Pam Bentson knew that she would have to work hard to help him develop a sense of dignity in his life. In the third grade, for the first time, he looked at me and said, "Mom, I'm different." He had never said that before and it was hard for her to hear. She said to him, "I love you Nick. You are different. It is different for you, but that's okay, because I love you, and we will find the right place for you to fit." As Pam told me this story there were tears in her eyes.

I have met many families who have confronted numerous obstacles yet have found the pathways to dignity for their children. Parents with older children remember the misconceptions that prevailed for many years: the "Refrigerator Mom" theory or the idea that Raymond in Rain Man was the embodiment of what it meant to have autism. Can you imagine hearing this diagnosis and at the same time thinking that you as a parent were somehow responsible for your child's disability? Can you sense the frustration of finding very little reliable information about a subject of such importance? Can you feel the despair of the parents having such scant resources to rely upon while at the same time being told that the prognosis for your child was grim? Thankfully, the times are changing for this generation of children and for their families.

What does it mean to lead a dignified life? How do parents help their children navigate in a world that isn't always sensitive to individuals with differences? Families recount how insensitive, uninformed, and distancing the community can be. When children, who otherwise look normal, have disruptive or unusual behavioral problems in public, strangers can be very unforgiving. Frequently, onlookers attribute the child's behavioral problems to ineffective parenting or to the child being a "bad seed." They often stand to the side rather than help, their faces full of judgment rather than empathy. Some parents have told me that, although it's difficult for them to admit, they wished at times that if their child had to be disabled, that the disability had taken a more socially acceptable form. Some parents make the decision to fully participate in activities outside the home no matter what the cost; others modify what they will attempt; while others retreat, saying that it's easier to avoid being ostracized. And of late, parents are beginning to tell me that they sense a greater understanding in the community—a more "How can I help?" rather than "What kind of parent are you and what kind of child do you have?"

Lack of acceptance and tolerance by classmates and neighborhood peers can compound the isolation of already sensitive children. Rather than being a haven of learning and friendship, school can be a place of bullying, scapegoating, and despair for the child with ASDs. There are too many stories of the child who finds himself all alone or mercilessly taunted.

But there are also stories of the children who find acceptance and develop the skills to form positive social relationships in settings that are designed to meet their needs. One parent told me that one of the happiest days for them and their son was when he had "real" friends to invite to his bar mitzvah. This was in stark contrast to the past, when for birthday parties and other celebrations his parents would call upon their family and friends to send their children to fill in for the friends that their child simply didn't have.

The issues of dignity are larger than life when parents weigh the decision to disclose to their child that he or she has autism. They question whether this disclosure is helpful or harmful: is it a label that limits their child or a label that will enable them to better understand their differences? Will lack of disclosure help to protect their child from slings and arrows that could be aimed at them by uninformed or insensitive peers, family and friends? Many parents have made the decision to be public and this decision has opened up the pathway to dignity for many children.

Teddi Cole remembers this decision. "Now, we're okay with the diagnosis. When Mary was first diagnosed, people said to us, 'Don't use the A word.' But that's sort of treating it like the Scarlet Letter. It's not the Scarlet Letter. Gary and I made the decision early on; we've talked openly in our house about autism for as long as I can remember. Mary knows she has autism. She knows that she's had a harder time doing things socially than other kids. So we felt that to pretend, not to call it by its name, would in the long run be harder for her and harder for us."

Parents tell me that they work hard to try to understand their children's inner life and unique expression of life. They try to grasp how their children experience those close to them and the world around them. In so doing, they have achieved tremendous insights—it is very different from what they imagined in the beginning. Some parents try to connect with their child through their child's perspective; others work to help their child conform to the world as they know it; and others try to meet in the middle to find a place of dignity and acceptance for their child.

In this time of greater public awareness, barriers to dignity are beginning to be dismantled and bridges to public acceptance, understanding, and help are being built. The powerful stigma that for many decades has limited dignity for those with autism is beginning to recede. Now we are speaking more openly: there is no shame, there is nothing to hide. Dignity and difference are not incompatible.

All of us need feedback in our lives that tells us we are valued, that we are accepted and we are loved. Let us work to tear down the barriers to the dignity that these children and families deserve. It is an important movement that has been long overdue whose time has finally come.

teddi and gary
cole

Mary Cole knows that she has high functioning autism. Her parents, actors Teddi and Gary Cole, made the decision to tell Mary, their family, friends and community about her autism and to speak freely about it. They believe that this candor will not only prevent stigma for Mary but will also contribute to reducing the stigma for others. As advocates in the public arena, the Coles are paving the way for other parents and supporting public policy reform. Their voices are loud and they are clear.

It's not the Scarlet Letter…

Teddi: We were sent to a developmental pediatrician who observed Mary for a while. Then she asked us, "What is your greatest fear?" I said, "My greatest fear is her self-esteem. I don't want her to feel that she's different from other kids. If she's got a speech delay, I'd like to be able to help her with that." The doctor said, "I need you to know that I'm leaning toward autism." And our brains just stopped. I remember getting into our car and shaking, because we didn't have any knowledge. It's like being thrown into the middle of the Atlantic Ocean and having someone yell, "Find New York!"

Gary: As soon as we started to get information, it got better: more information equals less fear. I went through a book looking for all the reasons why autism didn't apply to Mary. It was easier at that point to deny the diagnosis, but we started to do the work that needed to be done. We learned so much about autism and autism spectrum disorders. Mary was responding to all of her therapies, and autism became a part of who she was as opposed to something that needed to be cut out of her. Autism is as much a part of her as blonde hair—and we love every part of her.

Teddi: I remember sitting in Mary's room one day and trying to get her to engage with me in playing a game. And she didn't engage, she didn't want to engage, and I started to cry. I was feeling very sorry for myself because somehow in that moment it was about me. She turned around and said, "Mommy, you want a Popsicle?" which was a treat I'd offer her if she were upset. While I ate my Popsicle, I looked at her and watched her playing and I thought, "You know what? This kid is happy. She's okay. I'm the one that's unhappy." In that moment I realized that I needed to change the way I looked at her, I needed to meet her halfway. I needed to find out how she thought and how she viewed life, as opposed to trying to get her to completely see how we did things, trying to get her to do things our way. That moment freed me.

Now, we're okay with the diagnosis. When Mary was first diagnosed, people said to us, "Don't use the A word." That

seemed to make sense: we wouldn't want her to know that she had autism. But that's sort of treating it like the Scarlet Letter. It's not the Scarlet Letter. It's not a label; it's a diagnosis. When you have a diagnosis, you know where to go, what to do, how to work with whatever IT is. Gary and I made a decision early on: we've talked openly in our house about autism for as long as I can remember. Mary knows she has autism. She knows that she's had a harder time doing things socially than other kids. So we felt that to pretend, not to call it by its name, would in the long run be harder for her and for us.

Gary: She's named Mary after Teddi's mother, but we never thought that Mary Cole sounds like "miracle" when you say it fast. She is that.

sally and robert
calzada

Sally and Robert Calzada have two sons, Eric and Jonathan, who are just one year apart in age. Jonathan is seriously challenged by classic autism. With this diagnosis, they knew that the dreams they had for Jonathan had to change. Robert, who loved to play football and baseball and taught these skills to other children, had to face the reality that he would not be playing ball in the same way with both of his sons. Sally and Robert have tried to create as normal a life as possible for their family and have weathered the trials of their lives at home and in the community.

One smile erases a hundred tantrums.

Robert: I know my son has serious, serious challenges. His label is "very low functioning," he's non verbal, and he's eight years old. Jonathan's autism has changed us profoundly. I tell my other son and other people it's not just Jonathan who has

autism: we must think of it as the four of us who have autism. It doesn't stop when he's at school. It doesn't stop when he's asleep. It never stops. We realize that's the way it's going to be. All the tears, and all the anger and all the cursing in the world—and believe me there's that—doesn't stop the fact that you still have a job to do, and you have to wake up the next day and tackle it.

We're on display everywhere we go. We deal with it everyday constantly in the stores, in the malls. There are places we won't even try to go to—as a family we can't go to a movie theater. Sometimes we can't even go to a Dodgers game and that is one of the things that our other son Eric really enjoys. We tell Eric the truth, that his brother is different and that he needs special attention and that not all of these things fit in his life. Our dream is for our sons to enjoy their lives together as much as possible. We want them to do things together as much as possible, swim, ride bikes, but there are a lot of activities that are off limits for Jonathan. So we have to be very fragmented as a family. We have to split up—one of us will go with Eric and one of us will stay with Jonathan.

Sally: We don't want to just hide at home. We want him to know the world outside of the home too. So we take him to the supermarket, even though it's hard; we take him shopping for shoes and we take him to restaurants, and at least those things we can do all together, even if it's a little difficult. It is difficult. The community is unforgiving—every single person in the world is staring at us. When he was three or four, maybe they were a little more lenient with his behaviors and tantrums; maybe it was a bit more common to see a younger kid behaving like that. The older he gets, the less forgiving I think they are. It immediately puts you on the defensive.

Robert: As difficult as it is to have someone judge you, when someone is judging your child by a stare, a look, it does something to you. It's not a nice feeling. It hurts and bothers us. I've begun to lash out a bit more. I wish we could tell everyone that passes us, "My son has a disability. It's hard for him to calm down, and it's hard for him to be patient right now." I want them to give us some leniency in the line at the restaurant, here and there, because I don't feel we should be excluded from as normal a life as we can have. It sounds rough but I'm the most proud father in the world.

Robert: One of my favorite times of the day is when Jonathan is sleeping. I'll look at him and I'll look at Eric, and they are exactly the same. There's no difference and there's no ability or disability. I bought them both baseball gloves; I think when they were one or two years old. I've taught baseball and tennis all my life, but I can't teach one of my own sons.

But if you could see all his giggles and smiles, that's enough to make it through all the bad times. One smile erases a hundred tantrums.

mickianne
bradshaw

Mickianne Bradshaw learned her son James' diagnosis when he was two years old and she was pregnant with her second child. In the beginning, she knew very little about autism. In time, Mickianne developed her own understanding and acceptance of James and his high functioning autism. She came to the realization that autism does not define who James is—first and foremost, he is her beautiful boy.

Learning to love unconditionally...

All I knew of autism was rocking and flapping and sitting in the corner. I read an article in either *Time* or *Newsweek* that said autistic children look at their parents as if they're "flesh-covered bags." That's how they referred to it, and that's what I thought—and it was devastating. I remember sitting next to his little toddler bed and crying while he slept. It was like I was mourning the loss of the child I knew, and that went on for a while, and eventually, over time, I realized he was still the same.

James was still the same beautiful boy he had been before they told me he was autistic. Nothing had changed except for how I looked at him, and I had to fix that. As time goes on, you do. You realize you just have to roll with it. Now that I know who he is, it's nothing like what they said in the books—absolutely nothing like that. I can't imagine him any other way, honestly. He is who he is.

I had read that children with autism couldn't bond with their mothers; that if I left the room, he wouldn't care, as if I was just another object like a block. That was very scary, but it turned out to be far from the truth. He's a cuddly lovable child; he bonds with me. The main thing was that I wanted a relationship with my child.

We're very close; I'm very close to both of my children. I just grew with James. As I learned more, I let go of the "have to cure, have to make him better, have to make him like all the other kids." I started to embrace his odd behavior. There's so much push to make them normal, to put the square peg in the round hole; I don't think they belong there. For me, I know my son doesn't belong there.

If he wasn't doing as well as he is, I don't know how I would feel. Because this is an ongoing process: as he grows and I become more comfortable with who he is, as he continues to be successful at school and in the community—and he has friends now—I'm feeling more comfortable with who he is. This doesn't mean I'm leaving it here and stopping, or that we're not going to grow anymore. We are still working. He's still a kid—we have to fight to do his homework or make him participate in events. I think my definition of success is a lot different than it used to

be. There are things that still break my heart: when he talks about driving—and he talks about driving all the time—and what kind of car he's going to get. I don't know if he's going to drive. And that's a hard one to deal with, because that's his mission in life, right now at age eleven. For me, success for him is living on his own and having a job. I think he wants that too, and that's success.

You have to let go of the dreams you had when your child was first born. You have to accept who they are, and it makes you accept a lot of other things in life. I'm much more patient with people. The things that were important before, the material things, you realize how unimportant they are. It opens your heart to learning to love unconditionally.

dr. anila
guruji

Dr. Anila Guruji and her late husband Dinesh, an engineer, had always planned for their children to be highly educated and to excel in their chosen professions. They take great pride in both of their children, Neha and Anand, who have accomplished so much, each in his and her own way. They recognized that success is measured with different yardsticks and that Anand's achievements are truly remarkable. Anila is very proud of the fact that Anand, who has autism, is now attending community college.

There is no shame…

I knew that something was wrong with Anand. Every single physician I took him to said that there is nothing wrong with this kid. They even gave me the example that Einstein didn't speak until age six and a half. So why worry? But as a mother, I knew that something was going on—something was wrong.

When I received the diagnosis, I got the strength to carry on with it. It's extremely difficult to find out that your child has autism. Will he be lower functioning or higher functioning? Will he be able to go through his life in a routine way or not? And will he be self-sufficient or not? How will this affect my other child, who's only three and a half years older? I wasn't sure what was going to happen.

I had to explain to my husband that we didn't have a normal life now. Our life has changed. Our world is to help this child learn to be self-sufficient, to fit into society. And we have to do all those things to make sure that we can take care of him. So that's what we did.

At home he was upset, screaming and yelling. He was physically violent. He didn't understand what was going on. He didn't think that I was his Mom. I would say to myself, "I don't know how I'm going to handle him when he grows older. He's a big kid, I'm a small mother. He's five feet five, 200 pounds plus." But I always kept faith. I always fought for everything. I never took no for an answer.

Now he's a young adult, he has lots of energy, he's holding a job and he goes out into the community. I ask him every day, "What do you do?" He tells me exactly what he does. Everybody loves him at work; the Cambridge Farm people where he works called to tell me that they want to give him a full-time job. It's an amazing story, but he hasn't had a tantrum for the past five years. Five or six years ago, I didn't think that this would be possible for Anand. When he got his job at Cambridge Farms, it was the happiest moment for me.

I don't expect Anand to be genius or become a pharmacist or doctor. There is no shame in any kind of work that he does. Many friends and family members have asked me, "Why do you let him work in a place where he scrubs the floor?" I have no problem with it; there is no shame in doing *any* work. He doesn't

have to work, but I want him to. I want him to be self-sufficient and support himself as much as he can. My goal has always been to make him the best he can be.

If any other parent is reading this, I want to say never give up on your child. You always have to struggle, but just keep on going. The strength will be there with you.

pam
bentson-geyer

Pam Bentson-Geyer, a single mom for a number of years, has four children with a sixteen-year age span. She was the victim of domestic violence in her previous marriage and had to relocate her family. At the same time, she reinvented her career and became a lawyer after working as a nurse. When her third child, Nick, seemed to regress after the age of one, she knew that something was wrong, even though the pediatrician told her that he would grow out of it. Pam is a courageous and resilient woman who came to terms with what it means to have a child with high-functioning autism and what would help Nick to lead a happy life.

Mom, I'm different...

My child stopped talking. I can look at a photograph of Nick at age one and then at a photograph of him at age two, and there's a different child—I call it "the child behind the eyes." The social aspect of it was my child was not engaged.

There are a lot of parents who do deny, and they think that if they call it something different, or if they ignore it, it's going to get better. It's not going to get better if you go into denial. This is your child's life, this is the way it is, and the best thing that you can do is try to develop a quality of life so that your child has some autonomy.

If you're going to benefit your child, you need to get into his world, you need to understand where he's at. I think that really became poignant when my son in third grade, for the first time, he looked at me and said, "Mom, I'm different." He had never said that before and it was hard for me. I cried. That was the moment when I thought, "I have to deal with this. He knows he's different. You don't help your child by not accepting it." I said to him, "I love you, Nick. You are different, but that's okay because I love you, and we will find the right place for you to fit."

I decided early on that the disability wouldn't run our life. We would be a family no matter what the challenge was, so we did not stop doing what we were doing because of Nick's challenge. And was it hard? Absolutely.

The best resource is experience. People who have experienced what you are experiencing can tell you that the sun continues to set and rise and it's another great day. It's another great opportunity—for those ten steps that you took backwards yesterday, you can take two forward today. With Nick, I could have gotten lost in despair and said, "He's never going to do this or that"; and maybe he won't. But there's a lot that is positive that can happen.

I have fun with Nick. He can be extremely enjoyable to be around. It doesn't mean there aren't bad days; and for parents who begin this journey, there are rough roads. There are days that will bring you to your knees, and you're just going to look for strength from somewhere, whether it's from prayer or a companion. Or whether it's from just looking at your child and saying, "You came to me, and you picked me. I'm going to do the

best that I can for you." And that's how you survive. I just keep moving forward. I've always looked at it this way: whatever challenges are given to you in your life, you have to continue to look forward and take responsibility for the choices and decisions you make.

kathy and tony
peyser

Kathy and Tony Peyser's only child, Jeremy, is now a young adult. Jeremy has classic autism and grew up in a time when information and understanding about this disability were limited. As parents and writers, the Peysers recognize the importance of public awareness and look forward to expanding opportunities for special needs children. Tony has recently written a collection of poetry about his family's experiences with autism and is dedicated to heightening media sensitivity to disabilities.

A diagnosis doesn't change the child.

Tony: When we got the diagnosis of autism at UCLA for our son Jeremy, I had never felt at a lower point in my life. You've prepared for one life and now suddenly you're having another life. If you find yourself saying why me, the line should be, why not me! It's just the way of the world.

Kathy: I tell people who get this diagnosis that it's going to take a little while to come to terms with it and it's not going to be better in a week and it won't go away. It's devastating news and you can't just fall apart because you have a two-year-old who's running around and needs an enormous amount of attention.

Figure out which people in your life are going to stick with you; who you can call on the phone who will just listen on those days when you're having a hard time. Who will support you emotionally? Just kind of gather your emotional wagons in a circle. Find things that you can do to make you feel better after you're knocked down, to build yourself back up. You don't have the luxury of falling apart because you have a child who's depending on you.

Tony: There is nothing bigger in life to make you grow up than having a child, but if you have a child with special needs, you have to just completely focus yourself and get your priorities straight. The tangentials that you thought were really important, or certain expectations, those fall by the wayside and you reorient your life.

A diagnosis doesn't change the child. A child who has autism, is still your child. It doesn't mean that you have to love them less. Invariably you love them more.

Kathy: I just decided early on that I would focus on what Jeremy could do, not what he couldn't do. For Jeremy, the communication equipment that's becoming available has opened a world for him that didn't even exist for him a year and a half ago. You don't know what will be available in the future. Technology, ten, fifteen years from now could open doors and open up a world that isn't available now.

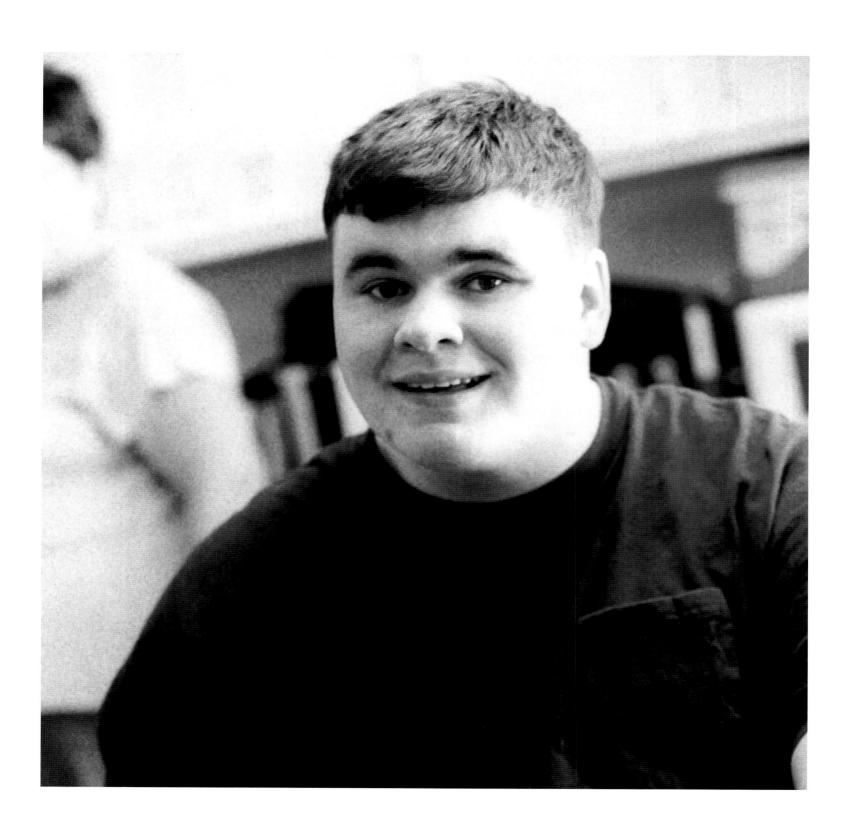

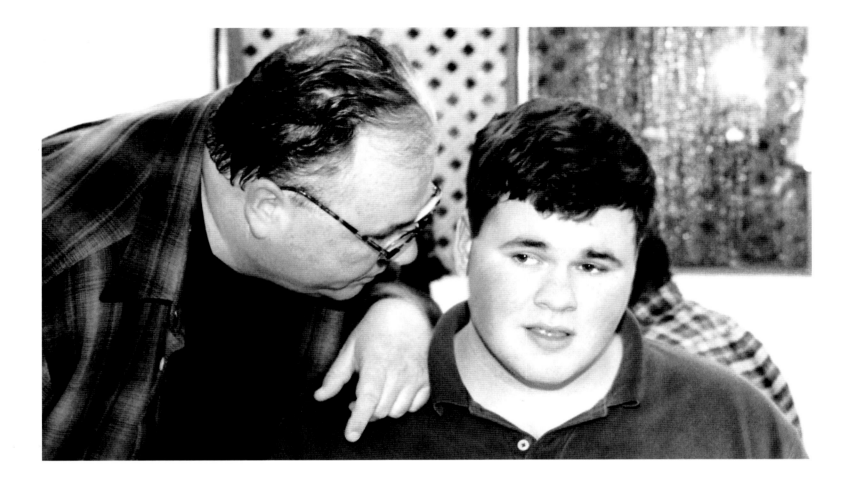

Tony: I think that children with disabilities are routinely mocked in the culture and in the media. I've written freelance commentaries about this for many years and I'm encouraged about the progress: I have contacted television networks, magazines, and they've changed things. On a TV episode, one character said to another in a joking manner, "Are you retarded?" At the end of the show, the remark was repeated and they all laughed again. I wrote a letter to the head of the network and they wrote back to me, "We have re-edited the episode. It will not air again with that word in the show." So it is possible to make that kind of change.

Kathy: I just want as good a quality of life for Jeremy as we are able to provide. He's a remarkable young man in a lot of ways.

He has a great spirit, a great heart and we just have to find a way for him to contribute to the world, because he can.

Tony: I remember once reading to Jeremy "The Cat in The Hat". The book starts, "It was raining and we had nothing to do." Then I improvised and said, "So, the two decided as soon as it was night, they would go outside and fly a kite." Jeremy was nodding off, but he looked up and pointed to the book, then hit the book as if to say, "Stay with the text, Dad." And I realized: he understands; he knows the difference. I think these kids can do a lot more than any of us—or certainly people who don't know them—give them credit for. That's what you have to look for.

sue and kenny
rosen

S ue and Kenny Rosen have two young children, Kyle and
Ivy, who both have autism. When they began their lives
together, Sue and Kenny could never have anticipated
what the future would hold for them. The Rosens have come to
terms with the reality of their children's challenges. They have
had to make many adjustments and have re-established the
priorities in their lives. Their goal is for their children to be
happy and to live as independently as possible as adults.

It warms my heart…that there's a place for my kids to learn.

Sue: Our children's autism drove us apart for a while—big time. I was just Ms. Angry and he was Mr. Denial. The two of us were walking on separate paths.

Ken: I do remember feeling like aliens—you could have shaved our heads. Sometimes that's how we felt, being looked at like four bald, little Martians in the world. It feels like that sometimes, but it's getting better.

Sue: If you would have told me ten years ago that I was going to be the parent of two autistic kids, I would have probably said, "just cut my head off—you're crazy, not me." Probably my biggest problem in life before I had kids with autism was my dry cleaning not being ready. "What am I going to do? My God, they said it was going to be ready Thursday and today it's Friday." The autism broke me down to realize what's important in life and what's not.

I have more faith now. I'm not as angry. I have learned to let go of the anger because the anger was killing me. It was just eating me up. If I wasn't angry at you and the world, I was angry at myself for being such an incapable incubator. So much bizarre, bizarre stuff went through my head. "What did I do wrong?"

Ken: I think our goals changed. Typical families think about the future and start saving for schools and colleges, cars and proms. And now, my goal is just for the kids to be happy and live independently. We won't be here forever. When I'm on my death bed, I hope to somehow get a sign from my kids saying it's okay, you can go.

Sue: My children's autism has brought us to a place in our lives where it's not about the outside, because they've taught us about the more primitive things in life: food, shelter and love. I also think that it gave us so much strength, but a little piece of me died inside too. There's that trade off.

Ken: A lot of people have asked me what causes autism. I don't live my life wondering what happened. I live my life with my kids wondering who can help them and what we can do. That's why I love their school because the school accepts the kids for who they are and what they have. I just love walking in the doors of their school because of the dignity that's everywhere in this school—from the teachers, how they teach the kids, and how the school is. It warms my heart to see what's happening and that there's a place for my kids to learn.

michel
gour

Joey Gour feels a great sense of pride when he plays with a band from his independent living skills program. Sometimes he plays on Sundays in the bakery that his parents Michel and Edie own. The Gour family, including their older son Jason, has been dedicated to helping Joey grow in his self-esteem. They are grateful that Joey has this ability to express himself in music, which gives him so much pleasure and so much positive feedback from those around him. As a young adult, he is happy and fully engaged in his life—a life that is productive and rewarding.

Music is Joey's life...

When we gave Joey his first guitar—just a toy guitar—he was rocking out, enjoying the music. Later on he had a real guitar, and he just started playing and practicing on his own. He started to make his own music, and he spent a lot of time practicing. When he was eleven years old, my older son Jason had a bar mitzvah, and Joey created a song—without words, it was just mumbling, there was no language—but the music was so beautiful. He played the song at his brother's bar mitzvah, and it was incredible, and then slowly, he got stronger and stronger in music.

When Joey's bar mitzvah came, we had to do something special for him. He could not do a speech, so we created something that had music. For the opening, he learned a song by Jon Secada. I told him, "You learn that song and you'll get another guitar." He got very excited and he learned that song. He had a beautiful, beautiful voice, and he opened the evening with the song. It was very touching, because a lot of my friends who knew him when he was a child thought they would never see such progress. And all of a sudden he's thirteen years old, and he opened with a beautiful song—with a beautiful voice, he walked amongst the guests, and came back on stage and finished. It was such a beautiful time. And then, he had a special song for each person who came up to light a candle.

Although he had tics in those times, everything was perfect. That evening, he performed all of the songs beautifully—and the next day his voice was gone. Sometimes, at thirteen voices change. He then learned to play the keyboard, took some singing lessons, and his voice was back again. Music is Joey's life—he's spent more time with music than anything else. And we're very proud of him performing in different places with the band from his independent living skills program. He's played in different places for three years.

Joey is thankful and appreciates us, and always worries about the future. He came to us once and said, "Dad, Mom, I don't know what I would do when, you know, when you're not going be around. Who is going take care of me?" I said, "That's why you go to a program. They teach you how to be independent. And don't forget you have a brother, who loves you very much, and he'll take care of you." It was very touching.

magdalena and frank
del olmo

B orn of migrant farm workers, journalists Magdalena and Frank del Olmo took great pride in their education. They had great aspirations for Frank's daughter, Valentina, and for their newborn son, Frankie. When he was diagnosed with high functioning autism, they were determined to help Frankie realize his fullest potential. Magdalena and Frank faced the challenge head on, and they decided to be public about the issues of autism.

If we can talk about diabetes screening and asthma epidemics, we surely can talk about autism.

When I first heard Frankie had autism, it was devastating. He's my only child, my firstborn. I had planned on having more kids, but as we learned more about the challenges, he became everything to me. And my husband and I pledged to find out as much as we could. We didn't go into counseling. We threw ourselves into learning as much as possible and figuring out what we could do to help him. Initially a lot of the literature that I read was outdated. It was the "Refrigerator Mom" theory that had been unquestioned for so long and cost us so much time in terms of the research that should have been going into autism. It was so disheartening. We were devastated and couldn't stop crying.

We both figured there had to be something somewhere out there to help our son. And luckily we found other parents who felt the way we did, who cared tremendously about furthering the pace of research and early intervention and educational curricula, all the things that could help rewire his brain while he was still young. The first time we heard people talking about hope, it wasn't the physicians; it was the other parents. Many of those parents had their kids at The Help Group; others were from Cure Autism Now. They really wanted to push science and research—and they first used the word *hope* with us.

Those first years after the diagnosis were about getting him early intervention and getting it to him quickly and thoroughly. And so began about six years of driving him to therapies: speech therapy, occupational therapy, and play therapy using the Greenspan model. Really it was an odyssey. We were averaging seven or eight thousand miles, driving all over Los Angeles County. You name it, we drove it. Our search was to put together all the best research-based approaches that we had found would help children with autism. It was physically fatiguing and emotionally difficult; it was hard on my son. When I think about

all those hours he spent in the back seat of a car being driven from place to place! We also worked very closely with our physician to look at medical treatments, diet changes, anything to help Frankie with all the issues that he had. For him it wasn't just autism: he also had asthma and allergies, and of course sensory overload, which is one of the hallmarks of autism. Everything is interlinked because if the kids don't feel good and if they're self-limiting in their diet—which Frankie was, like many children with autism—imagine all the things that their bodies are going through, let alone their spirit.

Both of us, using our journalism training and our research skills, found that the strength was in knowledge. The more knowledge we had, the more we could tap into education and the latest research. The more we learned, the more it was demystified, the more we felt very empowered to kick this thing. Frankie still has a lot of challenges; he still has autism and he will have it the rest of his life. We believe very strongly that the early interventions that we brought him made all the difference in the world—in helping him communicate and have more language skills and greater awareness of his soul and spirit. All those things made a big difference and have made his life so much richer and better.

Both of us made a commitment to share our learning with the world, to become public about Frankie's autism and not to hide it. Some parents don't want others to know about the autism and want to shield their kids from it. But if we can talk about kids needing glasses and diabetes screening and asthma epidemics, we surely can talk about autism.

There's so much to rejoice in, there's so much you can do to help your kids. Yes, grieve, but there's hope, so don't give up. What's important is education and setting goals for kids. Not just the goals that parents set with their educators in Individual Education Plan meetings, but the goals they set for themselves and their families. My husband Frank also had a background in management as well as journalism, and every January we would put together our list of goals and objectives, apart from all the milestones that the teachers wanted Frankie to achieve. Some of those goals and objectives were not medically, scientifically, or educationally driven. Some of them were to have more fun with Frankie in typical settings. Take him more to the movies, set up play dates with typically developing kids. Take him to

Disneyland more often. Explore new ways that he can learn. We wrote those goals up every year. This year it was help Frankie learn more about God. Help him learn more about what's really difficult for even typically developing kids to understand: spirituality, faith, the things that they can't see.

There's a lot out there for our kids—we're living in an exciting time. It's a time when so much has helped Frankie. There are current therapies that are research based and there are lots of wonderful, wonderful educational curricula that challenge the notion that our kids can't think and that recognize that they just think differently. And we just have to change our paradigm of thinking and try to see the world through their eyes and feel the world through their senses.

■　■　■

Several years ago, Frank passed away suddenly at the age of 55. He left a great legacy to his beloved family, Magdalena, Valentina and Frankie, and to the public. Recently a new elementary school in Los Angeles was named in Frank's honor. Frankie was very proud of his father.

■　■　■

Frankie's really blessed, and I think a lot of parents will be really blessed, because my husband was a journalist and he chose to write about the journey that we took with Frankie. In the last ten years, you couldn't talk about Frank del Olmo without talking about Frankie and the *Los Angeles Times* columns that Frank wrote about autism. It was a commitment that both of us made: to become public about Frankie's autism and to share our learning with the world.

Frankie had the most incredible dad. What a brain! My husband went to Harvard and had earned a Pulitzer Prize and an Emmy. He was very well known and respected in journalism circles. The first executive editor named to the *Los Angeles Times* masthead was my Frank del Olmo.

Frankie always knew his dad was special, because he would talk to Frankie endlessly about science, and dinosaurs, and all the things that his inquisitive mind would ask about. But it's funny, Frankie didn't realize that his dad was well-known in journalism circles until after he died. He asked me why there were so many people at the funeral, whether his father was famous. I said, "Well, a lot of people knew and loved your dad. He was famous, yes, among very smart people, among journalists." I explained that his dad left this incredible legacy. Frankie is now learning what the word legacy means, that when people die their spirit does go to heaven, but all their good works stay behind on earth for people to enjoy.

One of the things I've done since Frank died was compile a book of the columns that have been published in the 33 years he was at the *Los Angeles Times*.

In Frank's words, "This year I finally allowed myself to start dreaming about my son's future again." Although Frankie continues to struggle against the effects of autism, a mysterious neurological disorder, his improvement has been so steady that at times he seems a completely typical nine-year-old, right down to braces for his teeth and a growing interest in video games and the latest cartoon series (his favorite is *SpongeBob Square Pants*). I sometimes find myself musing about Frankie's future, but not with the concern and fear I often felt when he was first diagnosed six years ago. Now I can envision him achieving things once thought impossible for all but the most exceptional autistic children.

hope

■ Kip ■ Sweeney & Miller ■ Rufael
■ Gott ■ Sarkisian & Elkin ■ Kell
■ Katz ■ Lewis ■ Russell

It was preschool graduation day. The children gave their rendition of "If You're Happy and You Know It" in a loosely formed circle clapping their hands. It was an exuberant celebration—teachers spoke of the great strides that their students had made and how privileged they felt to have had the opportunity to work with them. Parents sat in the audience with tears in their eyes and smiles on their faces. They said that they were thrilled to see their children taking part in the ceremonies and grateful that their children had the benefit of a preschool program designed specifically for children with autism. They were thinking about what this day could foretell about their children's future. Was it an auspicious beginning that would lead the happy-ever-after story for their children, a future more promising for their children than they had dared to dream?

Autism and hope are no longer mutually exclusive. Parents want other parents to know that as difficult as the challenges of autism can be, there is hope. They have shared their thoughts and innermost feelings so that others may benefit from their experiences and look more positively toward the future for their children. Although they candidly speak about the challenges, they also speak about how they have been able to move forward and reclaim hope.

When a child is diagnosed with autism, the impact on the family is profound. Their equilibrium is disrupted and they are flooded with feelings of denial, grief, anger, guilt, blame and shame. As parents work through these emotions, they must simultaneously begin to redefine the hopes they had for their children's futures.

Denial is a powerful defense system. It can contain the anxiety that parents feel when they first suspect that their child is not developing normally. Their denial is reinforced when they seek guidance from professionals who more often than not tell them on their first visit or two, "Don't worry. Your child will grow out of it."

This interplay of denial and "don't worry" can give false hope and significantly delay early identification and intervention. When parents finally break through the denial and confront the diagnosis they describe feeling a tremendous sense of loss.

As difficult as this process can be, parents say that it does get better. They begin to cope with their feelings and to mobilize their efforts to get help for their children. Bob Kip said, "We felt pretty shocked and galvanized into action. You take in an awful lot of information all at once, and you have to start sorting out what sounds reasonable and doable. You can curse the universe, you can say life's unfair, and then after a while you conquer that." Parents try to gather as much information as possible and to seek resources in their community. They say that it is more demanding and draining than they ever could have imagined. But it is where hope begins.

Parents of children with autism hope, like all parents, that their children will be happy, secure, and productive and enjoy a sense of well being and acceptance in their community. Pepper Russell shares her thoughts: "We want Kahlil to be happy, and he is a happy little boy. We want him to have whatever resources he needs to reach his potential. And if his parents aren't around, we pray that there will be people around him who will love and support him in whatever it is he needs to be successful, happy and peaceful—the same things we want for all our children."

Children with autism spectrum disorders vary tremendously in the nature and degree of their challenges—no two children are ever the same. Parents begin to see that success for their child is relative to their child, rather than comparing them with other typically developing children their age. The developmental charts simply don't apply. It's not about what Tommy can do versus other children, but rather, what more is Tommy capable of doing relative to Tommy.

When parents see that their children are making progress, although that progress can be incremental and made in very small steps, it can be a source of encouragement. Jason Elkin sums it up when he says, "I know every parent appreciates their child, but we truly cherish every smile, every word, every emotion, and every personality layer that is unfolded. It makes you lean and press harder and find strength in places you absolutely never thought you could."

As parents press forward, they hold on to their hope as they search for the interventions that will make the difference. There seems to be no limit or end to what parents will do for the sake of their child's progress. Fact and fiction can become blurred, and parents can easily be swayed to a particular treatment no matter how unproven it may be. It can set parents on a seemingly never-ending chase to do the very best for their child. For most, it is a full-time unrelenting search that is variously fruitful or disappointing and discouraging.

Many find solace as well as answers in support groups. It is a safe harbor for parents who are new to the experience of autism to be in the same boat with people who have started their journey years before. In the groups they can freely vent their feelings to others who have been there themselves. They hear firsthand how different, yet how powerful a force that hope can be for these families.

Parents hope that they will meet the challenge and be able to do all that they can for their children. They hope that government and philanthropy will provide funds to accelerate progress in the field. Many become actively involved in promoting this agenda. As the pace of scientific research intensifies, and intervention strategies are further developed and scientifically validated, parents look forward to a time when they can broaden the boundaries of their expectations like the parents at the preschool graduation.

hilary and bob
kip

H ilary and Bob Kip are loving parents to their twin boys, Kenneth and Daniel, both of whom have an autism spectrum disorder. The Kips are positive and proactive and provide their children with all of the opportunities that their community has to offer. As parents they have mastered many life lessons and radiate a dignity that is an inspiration to others.

Know that it gets better.

Bob: When we received the diagnosis for Kenneth, Hilary cried. And the next year, when we had the bad news that Daniel was autistic, although less severe, I cried. We felt pretty shocked and galvanized into action. You take in an awful lot of information all at once, and you have to start sorting out what sounds reasonable and doable. You can curse the universe, you can say life's unfair, and then after a while you conquer that.

Hilary: Don't look to blame anyone or anything or any set of circumstances. I think seeking out blame for the predicaments or for the schools or programs that go wrong is not productive. You want to move on to something that does work. Never be embarrassed or afraid to ask questions. My late grandfather, who was a great man, said to never keep secrets because you never know where help is going to come from.

I've never been afraid to say my children have autism and explain the current situation, and it's amazing what kind of resources or suggestions have come our way—or just love and support—because we're open about it. Secrets don't help, and blame doesn't help. Being open and accepting also helps instill the children with some self-esteem. If the parents aren't embarrassed about who they are or what they do, then the children are not going to be embarrassed or self-conscious.

Our families, which include educators and psychologists, were responsive. The boys are very lovable, both very cute, affectionate and responsive. People seem to want to be with them and to help them, even if they were being difficult or having a hard time. That's not to say that we didn't experience tantrum behavior or feeding difficulties, things that get in the way of a family gathering or could potentially. But people were pretty sympathetic and accepting—and helpful. I think maybe because we didn't freak out, people didn't feel uptight around us.

Bob: One of the challenges is bringing the kids out into the community, just going shopping or whatever. It's a very overwhelming world out there for these children. There's all this sight and sound and movement and sensation. We try to get them out into the community very early on every weekend. All I can say is, do it when they're young because it doesn't get any

easier, and they learn, little step by step. You go in, someone has a meltdown, you leave; next time you come back, you spend a little more time.

Hilary: Find out what's fun for them and go with that. These boys are boys and they're a lot of fun. That's an important thing to remember. It's always challenging, but it's always an experience and an adventure. Go to a park; go to a museum; go to a restaurant—just little, quick outings. And be prepared to bail quickly.

Bob: Even at the movies. When we first took our boys to the movies, often Daniel would get up and leave when the movie started, so we all had to go. But now as a family we can go in and sit and enjoy a movie.

Don't expect it's going to go real well all the time, and be prepared to bail any minute, but get them out there because if it's too hard when they're two, it's going to be twice as hard when they're four, then six times as hard and so on.

Hilary: I know some parents feel intimidated when people in the community are looking disapprovingly. But I can't notice them; I'm too busy! I'm so focused on the boys, I can't even look away. I can't be worried. If it gets in anybody's way, we say, "Oh, sorry." I really don't have the time to notice what other people are looking at or thinking. You need to focus on your child, and do what you can to soothe the child and calm the situation. You need to help your child transition to the next thing. That's what's important; what the crowd is thinking isn't important.

Bob: The rudest person was at an airport, someone young who didn't have children. On the other hand, I can't tell you how many strangers have said, "Oh, I've been there." People who have children tend to understand. Typical kids have days like that too. We've had a month, even years of these days, right. Nobody comes up and says, "Well, if that was my kid, I'd smack 'em." We've never heard any of that, or, "You're bad parents because your kids are misbehaving." We've always gotten responses like, "Oh boy. I've seen that before."

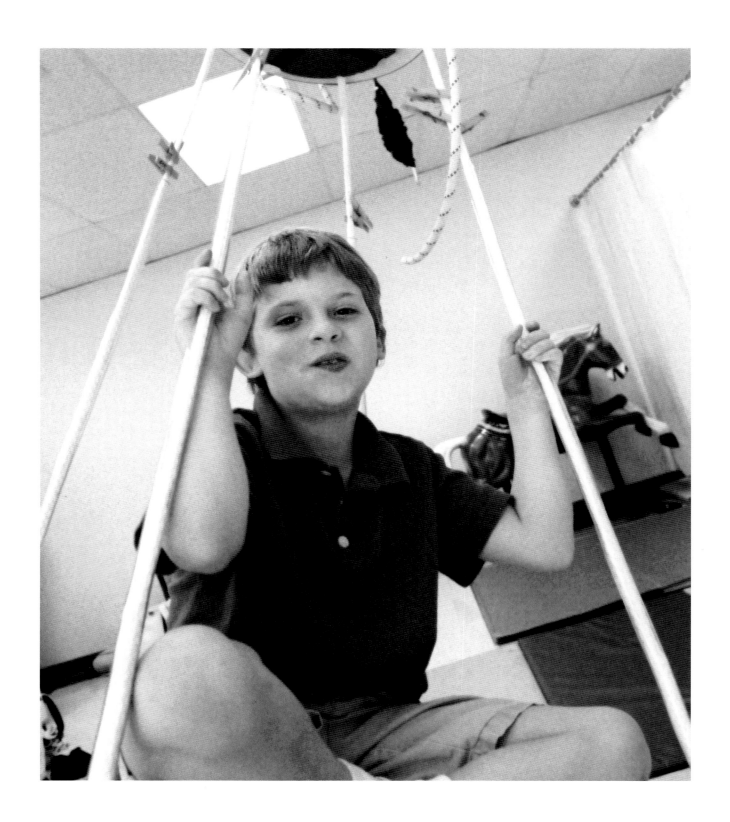

Hilary: Instead of being embarrassed you can just assume the other person's thinking, "Oh, I'm glad it's not us this time."

I'm not always calm: I can lose my temper, my cool, my patience, and my energy. The challenge of raising children with autism is very hard on a marital relationship; if there's not a clear bond to begin with, it's probably not going to survive. The support group is an appropriate venue for anger. You can vent and scream; you can say that life's unfair, and everybody agrees. And then, after a while, you conquer that. They'll talk you down and get you focused.

Know that it gets better; it does. Other parents of twins tell other parents of twins it gets easier. And we have more challenges, of course. It does get better; it gets easier; you do see progress. There's one really big tip I can give: when we talk about the progress we've made, I always try to look back six months. Where were we six months ago? Wow, this is a lot better than it was six months ago. Where were we a year ago, two years ago? As you look back you see progress and the giant steps you've made. You don't see it day to day or month to month, but if you look back at where you've been, then you see real progress. Those community outings that involve some embarrassment periodically, they get easier and easier. Navigating the school system becomes less Byzantine; it becomes less chaotic and peculiar. We don't take anything for granted.

Our children may have been born without enough tools to get through. We figure it's our job to help them get those tools and help them acquire those skills, and the good news is that it appears to be working nicely.

anne sweeney and
philip miller

Anne Sweeney and Philip Miller have two children, Christopher and Rosemary. Sensing early on that Christopher was not developing typically, they sought professional advice and began their quest to find the programs and services that would best meet his needs and nurture his potential. In this process, they recognized the value of parents sharing their experiences with one another to create a network of awareness, support and guidance. As a family, they speak openly about Christopher's autism spectrum disorder.

It's important to know you're not alone.

Phil: We noticed that Chris's speech was very delayed. He was two, or close to two and he wasn't really talking at all or even beginning to talk. We also noticed some difficulties with the way he was interacting with us and with others too. His eye contact with us seemed a bit off.

The pediatrician's response was, "He's a boy; they develop more slowly," and "The book hasn't been written on Christopher Miller yet. You're reading too many books about development." But that didn't stop us. We were either blessed or cursed with both having master's degrees in education and child development, so we knew that something wasn't progressing along the developmental chart as it should. We ended up getting a referral to a pediatric neurologist who put Chris through a series of tests and said there were some development issues that seemed to have a neurological basis.

Anne: In those days they called it "pervasive developmental delay," which was just a laundry basket term for any number of things. The only definite thing we had was the speech and language delay. We interviewed a number of speech therapists and the last question we asked all of them was, "Do you think he will ever speak?" And if they said, "I don't know," we said, "Thank you, good bye." And we just kept going until we found a therapist who said, "I have higher expectations for your son than you do." And we said, "Sold!" She came three times a week, in addition to Chris going to this therapeutic preschool, which had three kids, a teacher and two aides devoted to speech therapy and occupational therapy. It was a very intensive program.

Phil: As parents, it's the same kind of challenges you face with any child: finding the right schools, and providing them with the right environment in which to grow. Obviously, when you have a child with a diagnosis like autism, the challenges increase because it's difficult to find the right programs and the right support.

When we began, there weren't that many programs out there. Fortunately, now there are many more programs. Obviously, we

still need more programs and more room for kids within the programs that exist. At this point, there's really no reason as a parent to run from a diagnosis like autism. You really have to push hard, find the right education system, the right medical support, the best social support and provide the right home environment.

One of the things we learned along the way was the more open we were about what was going on with Chris and what was going on with our family, the more help we encountered. You have stories and strategies you can share with each other. Every contact opened yet another door for us. It was more help from another parent who was a few years ahead of us, who had been there.

We've become an informal clearing house for information: Have you tried this intervention? Have you been to a neurologist yet? What does your pediatrician say? Have you looked at schools? You feel like you're in the middle of helping to create a network of awareness and openness. We only learn if we keep talking to each other, and if we keep expanding this idea of family to be something very big, very productive, and very helpful to each other.

It takes a village to raise a child. With us it takes a thriving metropolis! It's important to know you're not alone.

zufan and kinfe
rufael

Zufan and Kinfe Rufael emigrated from Ethiopia to the United States. They have three young children: Emanuel, Lucas and Eden. Lucas and Eden, who are only one year apart in age, both have autism. The Rufaels had never heard of autism in their country. The diagnosis of Lucas came as a shock to them, but when Eden began to develop differently, they knew deep inside that their daughter had autism as well. With their abiding faith and both of their children in early intervention programs, Zufan and Kinfe have hope for the future.

You always have to keep the hope.

Kinfe: When they said autism, we said, "No, it can't be." We denied that this could be happening to our son, Lucas. It was hard—very hard. It's hard to believe, especially when your first child is normal. No-one on either side of our family has this. I had never heard of autism while I was growing up. They told us it was better to treat this at an early age.

At 15 months, our daughter Eden wasn't saying anything. So we didn't wait, we didn't deny it like we did with her brother. Before she was diagnosed, we knew inside that something was wrong. We just called the doctor and we took her to the regional center and now she's getting services.

Lucas was our first experience with autism. It's always true in human nature that you don't want negative things to happen. So we denied the diagnosis for a while; I didn't want this for my son. But deep inside we knew we had to do something about it.

We are a very religious family, so we just keep our faith, and we pray almost every day. We believe that through our faith we are going to get through this. We just keep praying.

Zufan: One thing I want to say is that hope started the first day we came to visit the school that Lucas would attend. In his school, we know that Lucas is safe, loved and very happy, and that gives us great hope. He knows what time to go in the morning—he can't wait to go to school. He pulls our hand and takes us to the front door.

When Lucas comes home, the first thing that we do is run, grab his backpack and read his teacher's communication book—what it says about Lucas and how he did at school that day. This is a blessing. We get to hear about him, we feel like we are next to him, and that's the major thing. The teacher tells us what we can do for him.

Since Lucas started school, he's improving; and seeing him happy and carrying his backpack and going to school, that's the hope we are happy with. And now, his sister, Eden has started the same school—now we have hope for her too.

cathy and jim
gott

Cathy and Jim Gott have two sons, Danny and Nicholas. Jim's oldest son, C.J., and Jim and Cathy's son, Danny, have autism spectrum disorders. With her firsthand experience with autism as a mother and stepmother, Cathy founded an organization serving children with autism and their families. Jim, formerly a pitcher for the Los Angeles Dodgers, dedicates a significant amount of his time to Cathy's endeavors, as well as to public awareness efforts. Together they are making a real difference.

...what comes out of it at the end is acceptance.

Jim: Being a major league ballplayer, I was really excited about having a son. Not to minimize the joy I had with my daughter, but I was anticipating the joy that I saw with so many of the players who were able to bring their boys out, wearing the team jersey with their family name on the back. I dreamed of my boy out there getting a head start on every other little leaguer in the world.

So when my first son C.J. was born, who was later diagnosed with autism, I lived in denial, I totally lived in denial. I was stuck in disbelief that C.J. was not perfect—I was just stuck there. I was waiting for the Ritalin pill to cure him. I was waiting for occupational therapy to cure him. I was waiting for him to wake up one day and act like a perfect little boy—not have seizures and not hit himself in the head or throw himself down. It was very difficult for my ex-wife to have two brand new kids—we have twins—and C.J., who was three years old at the time. A year later, after Cathy and I got married, my ex-wife called and asked if C.J. could live with us.

Cathy: I was 27 years old, newly married, and had no children of my own, but I saw this child struggling, and from a really good place in my heart I thought, "Maybe I can do something, come in and make a difference." I came at it from the place of "I'll fix it, I'll help," but inside I was really scared. I was terrified and too scared to be honest about how terrified I was, but I was overwhelmed with the responsibility myself.

Jim: The first night that C.J. came to live with us, we put him to bed like any typical three-year-old and he fell asleep. When we woke up the next morning, Cathy walked into C.J.'s bedroom and found the room turned upside down. The beds were off of the box spring. Everything had come out of all of the drawers, and there was a path of Desitin and baby powder all the way downstairs, all over the place. We followed that trail downstairs into the pantry and C.J., who was hungry, had pulled a lot of food off the shelves and was inside a cereal box, very happy. We were shocked and tried to laugh it off, but it wasn't a very funny thing.

Cathy: I sensed a need for safety immediately, and it was all hitting me, "Oh my God, this responsibility"—for a child who was non-verbal at the time, with a lot of tantrums and head banging. So I just dealt with one thing at a time, and the first thing was safety. That day we built a barricade at the top of the stairs so that I could sleep, without worrying that he would run outside or do anything to hurt himself. I wanted him to learn to come to me if he's hungry, or for other needs.

He had no diagnosis. "He's difficult," is what his mom had said. So we didn't know what was wrong; we just knew something was really wrong. His problems were fairly obvious, so we got the diagnosis quickly, within the first three months that he lived with us; and then started a lot of services, occupational therapy and speech therapy. Being so young and never having had children or even nieces or nephews, I don't think I even realized how off the mark he was. He was not doing any of the developmental milestones that children do at three, the most basic goals: to sit in a chair, to hold a fork, to express anything appropriately. Very intensive intervention started immediately, even before we got the written diagnosis. Positive results from this early intervention were seen instantly; it was very quick.

Jim: I lived in denial until I had my second child with autism, our first child for Cathy and me, Danny, who is six years younger than C.J. I lived in a fantasy world with baseball and I just stayed in that and, as long as I was performing and doing what I was doing, I deferred everything to Cathy and saw that Cathy was holding up at home.

Danny came around and I saw him doing things that C.J. never did. I was thinking, "You're crazy. He's not colicky, he is not uncomfortable, he's not doing anything self-abusive." So I lived in that denial and bucked up against my wife and just thought she's just being oversensitive.

Cathy: C.J. was great prep for when our son Danny was diagnosed. At least I had a road map. I knew what I needed to do, and I had a team of experts who knew more about it than I did—but it was different emotionally when it was my own child.

Danny's story was very different. This is how autism is: no two stories are alike, there are commonalities, but they're all so different. I remember thinking, "What did I do in my pregnancy?", and feeling guilty; I beat myself up and down and went through my own denial. I think it's a normal, healthy response to grieve and to feel fearful, overwhelmed, and to be sad. But what comes out at the end of it is acceptance.

I can sit and be a victim and say woe is me, or I can look at it in a much healthier way—that this is my life and it is not a bad life, don't feel sorry for me. I have a great life, and yes, C.J. and Danny have autism—it takes a lot of work and a lot more patience than children who are typically developing. I'm okay and my kids are great and they bring a lot to my life.

Jim: I'm just coming out of isolation. I've been able to have a wonderful example with Cathy, just being able to see her openness. I work at Cathy's office and I get the chance to see about 100 kids a week working and assisting in a social skills class and it's wonderful. I've developed so much friendship and joy with the other families—I am so excited to go to see these kids.

jennifer sarkisian and
jason elkin

Jennifer Sarkisian and Jason Elkin were asked to remove their son Jared from two regular education preschools and one autism preschool due to the severity of his behavior. Unwilling to give up hope, they found a new therapeutic preschool and enrolled their son. In this program, Jared has made a great deal of progress. Although no longer married to one another, Jennifer and Jason are devoted to their son Jared and his well-being. His ongoing growth and development encourages them to look forward to a bright future for Jared.

History's full of stories of parents doing superhuman things where their children are concerned.

Jennifer: There was no one in either of our families who had been autistic or had been challenged with any kind of learning disability. For us it was some word that appeared in a movie with Dustin Hoffman; probably the extent of our knowledge of autism was having seen the movie "Rainman." Beyond that it was something that we truly had to educate ourselves in.

Jason: In doing the research and finding out that there were options, there were things that could be done—and then looking at all the data that said if you catch it early, and you do something about it, there's a really good chance that you can resolve the situation to a large degree—that was the genesis of hope. We realized that the 60/40 chance that we can do something about it is better odds than you get in Las Vegas. So we thought, okay, it's possible to do this, it is possible! It's a huge challenge, it's a daunting challenge, but it is something we can do.

I think history's full of stories of parents doing superhuman things where their children are concerned. I know that we don't feel particularly strong and that some of the things we've done perhaps have amazed us. When your child's concerned, you really don't know the extent of your ability. It's a very selfless pursuit of a goal, but it's the most gratifying experience of our lives.

Jennifer: When your child's involved, you just do it. There are times when it's very difficult and you just don't know where else to go or what else to do. You go to sleep at night and you wake up the next morning, and you've just got to press on and keep doing it. When Jared runs up to me and says, "I love you Mommy," and puts his arms around me, it's absolutely worth it. And you find those little things in every day that tell you that it's worth it.

Jason: As parents, I think we appreciate Jared more. I know every parent appreciates their child, but we truly cherish every smile, every word, every emotion, and every personality layer that is unfolded. It makes the effort worthwhile. It makes you lean and press harder and find strength in places you absolutely never thought you could.

Once he got to The Help Group, everything changed for Jared. We found our son. The behavior that we had been told would be a permanent obstacle to him being educated at any point in the future immediately started to subside. His communication improved; it was as if someone had turned a switch on in him, one of those sliding dimmer switches that once activated just kept on getting brighter and brighter and brighter. His personality and his happiness developed. Having all those things come together was just incredible! There aren't words to describe it: ecstasy, elation, joy, happiness; it's a miracle.

Jared received the Student of the Year award, and he was so proud! He understands what it is to work hard at school, what it is to succeed. He understood that it was a significant accomplishment for him. He sat there holding the award in his arms, saying, "Daddy, I'm Student of the Year; I'm Student of the Year, Daddy!" He was just beaming with pride and self-satisfaction. He had worked really hard and accomplished something that he knew was significant and not an everyday event.

Jennifer: For me he is becoming a typical child more and more every single day. The joy in his face and how happy he feels just bring me to tears. The changes that we have seen in him since he's been here were things that I never thought would happen.

Jason: He is making goals; he is personally striving more and more each day, with a greater sense of self and awareness. He has expectations for himself now, and I want to see him achieve them, all of them. I want to see him live the life that everyone told us was impossible, that we know now is not impossible. I want him to be able to stand up one day to a dumbfounded crowd and say, "I was autistic. They told me I was hopeless; they told me that what I'm saying to you right now was not possible. They told me that going to college and living a full life was not possible. And you know what? They were wrong." Maybe it's a slightly selfish dream on my part, but Jared's got a good heart, and I've got no doubt that he's going to want to help other children in the future, help them beat this, the way he's beating it.

kristina and justin
kell

K ristina and Justin Kell decided shortly after their son,
Norton was diagnosed with autism at two and a half
years of age to vigorously pursue intervention
programs for him. Even though Jason was not convinced that
Norton had autism, the Kells proactively sought services for their
child. Today, Norton's diagnosis of high functioning autism is no
longer in question, but more importantly he has made
significant progress in his development.

…I think Norton will be able to live a life that I didn't know was possible when I first heard the word "autism."

Kristina: When Norton was about four months old, we started going to a baby group. There were five or six other moms and their babies. Right from the beginning, Norton was different than all of the other babies in the group. All of the moms would be sitting in the group, talking and laughing, and I'd be in the back of the room trying to comfort Norton. He was not fitting in.

Justin: The director of the group introduced the idea that there could be something neurologically wrong with Norton. My first reaction was that I just assumed that there was nothing wrong. I put a wall up immediately. I think that deep down both of us knew there was something wrong. Norton just wasn't developing the way that he should have been.

Kristina: After four or five months in the group, he still wasn't hitting the milestones like the other kids. At this point, the director said that Norton might have autism.

Justin: I said, "Take Norton out of there"—I thought that they were jumping the gun. He made eye contact—that was one of the big things, I thought. I only knew about the severe form of autism. I didn't know about the spectrum, the different levels of autism. We didn't know anyone who had an autistic child.

As more diagnoses of autism were given to Norton, we took the approach that we had better try to get everything available to help him as early as possible. If Norton didn't develop, we'd never know if it was our fault for not trying.

Kristina: When we told our families, they were concerned and they wanted to get into action. I think they reacted better than we did. They were very supportive. I didn't want to tell anybody else. I didn't want him to be painted with the stigma of autism.

My initial understanding of autism was different than it is today. I thought Norton was going to have a disability his whole life, and in a certain way he will. But I think Norton will be able to live a life that I didn't know was possible when I first heard the word "autism."

Justin: Now I see that we have a family. We have Norton, and even with his diagnosis, he is a sweet child, he's a loving child. We have another child, our two-year-old, Hank. Our life goes on, and our family grows, and Norton's autism is part of who we are. I don't think of Norton as autistic, I just think of him as Norton.

Kristina: There was a particular day that was very hard for me with Norton. I felt very sad inside and really down. Norton still wasn't speaking very much. He was a little over three. I tucked him into bed, and he looked at me and said, "It's okay mama, I love you." I was shocked on two levels—that he knew it was a particularly sad day for me and that he could and would say "I love you." On another day, we asked him who his friends at school were and he actually could name two or three friends. Other people take moments like this for granted, but we don't.

Justin: The most important thing that I can tell parents is not to be afraid of the diagnosis. Get whatever help is out there. Services are not easy to find, you really have to do your homework. It gives us a lot of satisfaction to know that we didn't put our fears ahead of his being able to receive the therapy and intervention that he needed. I don't think that Norton would be where he is today without his special school. I'm sure of it. And now I really understand the benefits of early intervention. I think the fear is gone for me. I think that Norton is going to be all right.

illana
katz

I t's been nearly 20 years since Illana and David Katz's son, Seth, was diagnosed with high functioning autism. It was a time when the term was still relatively unknown, but they were committed to securing every opportunity possible for Seth. Throughout the years, they have appreciated every step forward that he has taken. With wisdom and sensitivity, Illana has co-authored several books related to autism.

If I had a dream it would be that he could lead a productive, happy life.

I knew when Seth turned two that his speech wasn't nearly as good as I thought it should have been, that there was something going on with him. So I started going to libraries and reading. I had a feeling he suffered from some kind of autism. I had seen movies of people working with autistic children when I was an undergraduate in college, and I thought he kind of looked a little bit like some of those children, but not totally like them. By the time he was three, I started taking him from doctor to doctor to doctor.

Of course at that time there was no high functioning autism diagnosis—it was just beginning of it; so I got different things. One doctor said there was nothing wrong with him. Then I took him to another doctor who said he's aphasic with some autistic-like features. Another said he might have autism, all the way down the line. Finally I took him to UCLA, where someone said he did have autism but he was high functioning. And that's the first time I ever heard the term "high functioning autism."

But it wasn't in any books yet. You couldn't find information on it. It was just like autism but not as debilitating. And that's how we started.

When my husband and I were we were told face-to-face that our son had autism, even though I had known in my head that this was true, it was probably the most difficult moment of my life, and I assume in my husband's as well. You just felt totally drained, totally numb, and that it couldn't be happening to you. But it was.

I was no youngster when I gave birth to him. How was I going to make the world okay for him if something happened to me or to my husband? I was totally perplexed. I was depressed, I'm sure.

You have choices. What are you going to do about this situation? You could do nothing and let the world put on the show for you. Or you could become involved and be in control and start deciding. I knew that underneath there was a bright little boy, and I was going to fight like the dickens to bring him

out, so that if something happens to me or my husband or both of us, he'll still be able to function within this world. That's right when I started to fight back.

I found out everything there was to know about any service that was available: where it was; how we could get it; what we needed to do; who we needed to talk to—and on and on. I spoke to organizations that put me in touch with parents whose children had been diagnosed maybe a year or two before. They told me what they had gone through, and that gave me hope. We started going to meetings with people who had children similar to and in the same age group as my own son. That's the way we started out. Later on I wrote a book—in fact, now I have two books out about autism. Our son has changed our lives completely. Just beautiful things have come from our son.

Every parent has to reinvent the wheel. Every parent has to do the same legwork.

It may be easier now, but it's still frightening, and you still have to navigate in a way that's most appropriate for your child—whatever level of involvement he may have.

If I had a dream, it would be that he would be able to hold a job and lead a productive, happy life. So that's the goal and that's the dream. How will the dream play out? We'll have to wait and see. But that's our real goal. I want to give him every opportunity that we, my husband and I, can find for him. But also those that he's able to take advantage of himself as well.

I think when you open the door in the morning, and you look at the world with the fresh morning air, you take a nice deep breath and you think, "Wow, look at the world I live in!" Not the geo-political world, but this moment. This is all we have, the moment, the day-to-day moments. And if you gauge yourself that way and move forward, you have success after success.

It's the little things that make a difference. Each new thing that your child does is cause for excitement and for thanks. I'm grateful.

emmie and richard
lewis

Emmie and Richard Lewis have two children, Brandon and Samantha. Brandon has autism and has not developed the skills to communicate verbally. Two years older than her brother, Samantha is a warm and loving sister to Brandon. The Lewis family is dedicated to providing the opportunities to help Brandon unlock his potential. Richard and Emmie poignantly share their experiences.

For anyone to say that there's no hope, doesn't make sense.

Emmie: In the beginning, Brandon was actually babbling and talking a little bit. We went to Israel when he was 18 months old and when we returned home close to his second birthday, his speech stopped and he began to isolate himself more. Something didn't add up. We weren't sure that he could hear. But when I would sing to him his favorite lullaby, "When You Wish Upon A Star," even if it was in a very low tone, he would look at me.

Richard: We had him tested. The doctor said that he could definitely hear. Before we went for an evaluation by a developmental pediatrician, I had read the *Newsweek* article on autism—I knew that Brandon was autistic. The doctor told us the diagnosis and I had a delayed reaction, I went home after the appointment, and probably cried for two hours. Everyone was in denial. We didn't tell my parents, but my mother had read the *Newsweek* article too—she knew, and she sent me the article.

Richard: Brandon has a sister, Samantha, who is two years older. She's very remarkable—she's never complained about not being able to do certain things because we couldn't include Brandon. She's so maternal and she loves him so much. The only thing that she ever complained about was that Brandon didn't pay enough attention to her at times. He does now, but he didn't when he was younger. At Sunday school they asked the students to write down something to thank God for. And she wrote down, "I thank God for my little brother."

Emmie: I remember when all of the girls in her class had to make a special wish. Samantha said, "I wish my brother would talk and say my name." And sometimes she explains it to her friends, "You know my brother has special needs, so it's hard for him to understand and learn." She says, "I'm teaching him to talk." As soon as his therapist leaves, she comes in and she teaches him; she plays with him and, they dance together. She tries so hard.

Richard: If you offered me the choice of a billion dollars or just to hear Brandon say, "Dad," I think I'd go for his saying "Dad." I'm afraid sometimes. I'm almost afraid to hope. It's just so hard. I dream all the time that he can say something—that he can talk or say, "Hey Dad, come here, look at this."

There's so much pain bottled up inside of me as a father. I'm not expecting Brandon to go to Harvard, but I have expectations that I might be able to play catch with my son, and that I might be able to teach him how to hit a baseball or throw a football. To me those are dreams now.

We know that there are lots of things going on inside him. We just have to figure out how to unlock them. It's going to take a lot of trial and error, but somewhere out there, there may be interventions that will work for him. We still don't know what causes autism. There are so many unanswered questions—for anyone to say that there's no hope, doesn't make sense.

pepper
russell

Pepper and Clifford Russell have four children. Their son Kahlil has an autism spectrum disorder. Although Kahlil's challenges brought changes to their lives, they persevered and secured the resources that could enable Kahlil to make progress. With the number of children being diagnosed with autism spectrum disorders on the rise, Pepper recognizes that services have not kept pace with the demand and that public policy needs to change.

It's not the monster in the closet anymore.

I feel somewhat blessed to live in this day and age because there's so much more information than ten years ago, or even four or five years ago. Unfortunately, the resources are not catching up with the demand. I think the general public is much more aware of autism. There's a lot more publicity; I've seen more articles and television coverage. There are more studies going on, and research.

Families shouldn't look at the diagnosis as the end of the world. Once you've sat and cried, the best thing you can do is to find out everything you can! The earlier you get help, the better your outcome will be. It's not the monster in the closet anymore.

When we had our first son, Clifford Nile, I still tried to do everything the same—I tried to live my life at the same pace. And then you figure you can't because with a baby your life is different. So you have to surrender to it. After we had Kahlil and he was diagnosed with autism, we had to surrender to what that meant as well. Our life would be different than we'd imagined. We have to meet our children where they are, disabled or not. Whatever lifestyle change comes your way, you have to roll with it

We want Kahlil to be happy, and he is a happy little boy. We want him to have whatever resources he needs to reach his potential. And if his parents aren't around, we pray that there will be people around him who will love and support him in whatever it is he needs to be successful, happy and peaceful—the same things we want for *all* our children: Ashley Marie, Clifford Nile and Cayenne Faith.

We started a small non-profit organization to raise money to help subsidize therapies for children with autism. A lot of therapies have been eliminated or made financially unobtainable due to budget cuts. Kahlil was affected by it. He was making great progress with his motor, communication and social skills in a gymnastics program for children with special needs and we had to take him out. It broke our hearts. We would like to help other children that are in the same predicament, to fund equestrian, music or art therapy, or whatever parents find work for them.

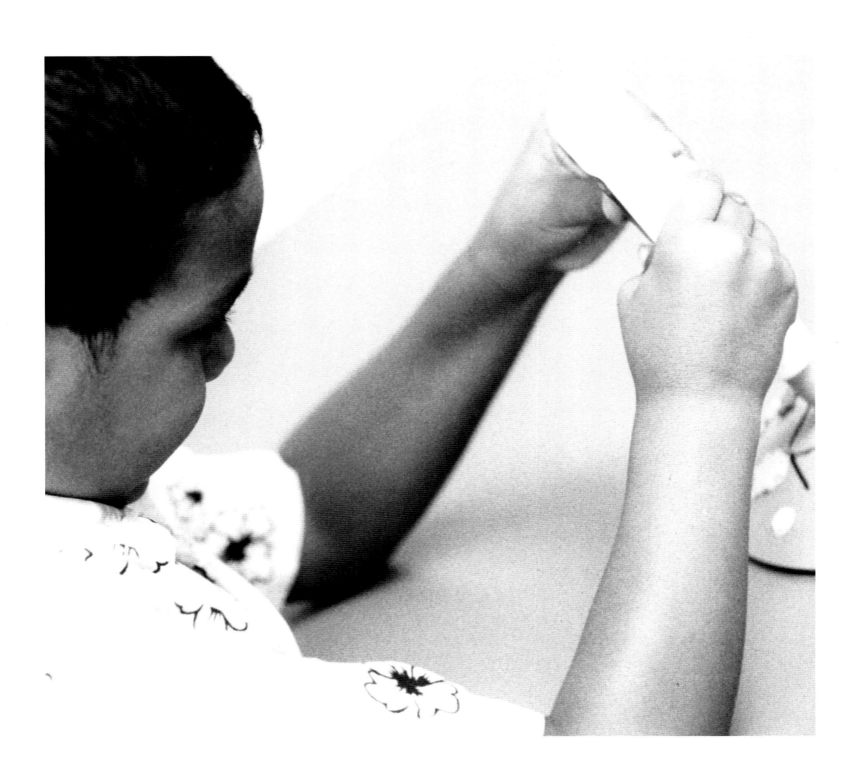

If I could speak to policymakers, I would say, "The number of children affected by autism speaks for itself. This is a vast community of people that we will have to deal with in the future. Right now, they're children, but in ten years they will be adults. There are all these children out there and many of them are not receiving the educational and therapeutic resources necessary to prepare them to function as independently as possible in the future. Radical changes need to be made."

opportunity

■ Jacobs ■ Vismara ■ Cervantes
■ Palmer ■ Fils ■ Emanuelli
■ Urquhart ■ Shapiro & Sharif
■ Green ■ Hartman

We have begun a new era of opportunity for children with autism. Although there is much yet to uncover about autism spectrum disorders, there is an ever-expanding body of research that better informs our ability to identify and educate these children. Armed with this information, an increasing public awareness and the growing demand, more programs are being developed to enable children to more fully realize their potential.

We recognize that effective programs now incorporate evidence-based best practices for diagnosis, education and treatment. We acknowledge that strategies must be tailored to meet the unique needs of each child. There is no single approach—no one size fits all—and we know that intervention can take place in different settings: in mainstream environments, special day classes, after school programs, clinics or in the home.

The times have changed significantly from the early days. When autism was first described by Dr. Leo Kanner in the 1940s, it was considered to be an unusual and infrequently occurring disorder. Information was scarce and the disorder was shrouded in mystery and stigma. Families had extremely isolative experiences that were compounded by misdiagnosis, no diagnosis, and lack of autism programs in schools and other community-based settings. Parents struggled to do their best for their children but more often than not had no viable options. State institutions became the homes for many children whose degree of disability could not be managed at home in a community devoid of opportunities. The goal was very basic—it was to warehouse children where their basic needs could be met with a degree of safety and security. Sadly, without the benefit of scientific and practical knowledge to fuel the development of other alternatives, this situation continued for several decades.

Nearly 30 years later, in the 1970s, the stage was set for significant change and for the evolution of meaningful opportunities for children with autism. No longer did we look to psychogenic theories and approaches. It was the advent of behavioral therapies and a science-based agenda to uncover the causes of autism and to develop effective assessment and interventions. Isolation, castigation, institutionalization, and "Refrigerator Moms" began to be set aside, and the field focused on efforts to create the opportunities that could transform the lives of children with autism. While much more promising than what existed and what we knew before, there was a very long way to go.

Today, we are still on the path to fill in the gaps and to accelerate the agenda of science and effective clinical and educational practice. Nearly every family I have met has had a difficult time in finding the help that could give life to their hopes and dreams for their children. The history of autism is filled with the stories of parents searching for the answers for their children—searching for opportunity.

Throughout the years, there have been many parents who, when confronted by the lack of opportunity, have taken it upon themselves to bring about positive change. There are the parents who have started grass roots movements to advocate for services, the parents who have established organizations beginning in their living rooms to raise their voices to demand and promote public policy change and to raise the dollars to expand research and quicken its pace, and the parents who have developed networks of support and information for other parents. Their courage and unflagging efforts have flown in the face of a world that was not changing rapidly enough to give their children the chances that they needed. The impact of their impassioned efforts is reminiscent of Margaret Mead's insightful words:

"Never doubt that a small group of thoughtful, committed citizens can change the world. Indeed, it is the only thing that ever has."

As the parent movements were developing, so too were the science of autism and the development of evidence-based educational and treatment best practices. School, clinic and community-based programs began to expand, as well as efforts to promote public awareness. At the same time, there has been a proliferation of unproven theories and treatments. Parents must be vigilant in their quest for the most appropriate services for their children.

Autism is not the dead-end diagnosis for a child that it was once thought to be. We now know that children with all forms and degrees of autism can make varying degrees of progress with a big "if"—"if" given the opportunity. There is a big difference between what a parent confronted in the past compared to what they confront now. We are no longer living in a vacuum of information about how to meet the needs of the children, yet the availability of services has not kept pace with the demand. Some parents speak about the significant delays of the diagnosis, in many cases years long. They share how frustrating it is to finally have the diagnosis, and to know that there are programs that could help their children but that these programs either do not exist in their communities or are not financially accessible to them.

The Cervantes family remembers their son's negative experiences in school. After years in programs unable to help their child, who has Asperger's Disorder, they were able to find the specialized program that focused on the social skills that their son so desperately needed. They are thrilled that he is finally in a program where he has found happiness and acceptance and is developing important social skills. However, they lament the many years of failure and isolation that he endured. They look forward to a time when all families can access the services that can have such a significant impact on the well-being and future of their children.

In contrast, there is the story that the Palmers, the parents of a young child with autism and two other young sons, tell. They speak of the rocky start, but then they speak of the significant progress that their child has made with intensive early intervention. "He's a very much, happier child now... Who knows where he would've been if we hadn't had him in an early intervention program… He understands what love is, and he understands being happy and how fun it is to play with his brothers. All of those things are new to him." In their own words, "Early intervention has given us our child back."

The demand for access and opportunity has become the rallying cry of parents, scientists and clinicians who are working hard to ensure that children have the programs and services that can make the difference—the difference that can be made for many children with early identification and intervention; the difference that can be made with educational programs that help children build essential skills; the difference that can be made by providing adolescents and young adults with the resources to enable them to function with the greatest degree of independence as adults.

Clearly, the research, clinical and educational work and advocacy must continue to grow and be translated into effective practices and public policy. It's time that we acknowledge that children don't fail; it is the systems of care that fail to give them the opportunity to succeed. The opportunity agenda must ensure that every child with an autism spectrum disorder, irrespective of where they live or the socio-economic status of the family, has the benefit of the best education and treatment available today.

If I turned back the clock to ten or 20 years ago and recounted the parents' experiences, the stories would have been far less hopeful than they are today. If I were to speak with parents ten years from now and ask them to share their experiences, I hope that they would recount all of the opportunities that were readily available that helped their children to develop the skills to lead dignified, productive and rewarding lives.

cheryl
jacobs

For many years, Cheryl and Jake Jacobs sought the correct diagnosis for their son Aaron. After having received many misdiagnoses, they were finally told that their child had Asperger's Disorder. They decided to move from Michigan to Los Angeles so that Aaron could have the benefit of a program designed to meet his specific needs. Although this was a major life change, they are very glad that they pursued this path.

We would do whatever it takes for our child to have a life.

When Aaron was 11, I read the book *The Mind and the Brain*. It was written by a doctor at UCLA who was doing research on Obsessive Compulsive Disorder and mapping of the brain. Aaron had been diagnosed with OCD when he was six. My husband's cousin was visiting from Los Angeles, and her husband was a therapist at UCLA. We met for lunch, and I told her what was going on with Aaron and about this book, that I wanted to have Aaron seen at UCLA. She said that she would help me. She called the following Monday with an appointment. Aaron and I were on a plane Thursday from Detroit.

Aaron was admitted to the UCLA Semel Institute Friday morning. This is where it got really intense for us, because, quite frankly, I didn't really know what we were getting into. I had never been in a psychiatric hospital before, and we started walking through locked doors, doors that had to be opened in front and locked behind us. They immediately took Aaron away.

You know your child better than anyone. If you think there's something wrong, don't hesitate to look into it—go after it, don't give up, and keep searching. We've been through so many detours. It took us 11 years to get to Asperger's. At any point we could have stopped and we wouldn't be here, and I don't know where Aaron would be.

For about 24 hours he was a mess, and it was just hell. Every time I went to see him, he would just hang on me and beg me to take him out. It was awful, but I had a lot of support from the staff at the hospital, talking to me about how he was when I wasn't there—which was actually quite fine.

What happened next was fairly miraculous. He settled in, and he started to hook up with the kids on the floor. He started to behave in a way that I hadn't seen in a long, long time: he relaxed. There was space around him. All of that stress and tension just rolled off him. Due to the structured environment, he knew exactly what would happen every minute of the day, and that helped him to just let go.

We had a meeting with the hospital staff, and they went through all their different assessments, and finally the word "Asperger's" surfaced. They just said it and kept going. I heard it, paused, and said, "Did you just tell me that he has Asperger's?" They said, "Yes. How do you feel about that?" I said, "Honestly, I don't have any reaction to it at all, because we've had so many labels put on this child. All that I'm aware of at this moment is that the way you've described him through your evaluation sounds just like him. You've hit on who he is—all of his little idiosyncrasies." Since he was six years old, we have spent all of our time trying to figure out where he fit in and what was going on with him. He just never fit in, and he's never been a really happy person. Anyone who has had this experience will understand our mindset: we would do whatever it took for our child to have a life.

We're spiritual people. That's my foundation. I just have a larger view of life, in terms of its context. One of the things that I talk to Aaron about a lot is that it's not what happens to us, but it's how we respond to and deal with it that moves us forward. We create the life that we want. Jake and I agreed that there's nothing back in Michigan for Aaron, but there are specialized schools here in Los Angeles, and we decided to move.

The teachers at his new school know what they're working with. The children are acknowledged and supported. People there are helping them deal with what they struggle with, so they struggle less tomorrow. Aaron's much more inclined now to see that there's more than one way to do things, that there are possibilities. He had never had a positive school experience, never in eleven years. This was the first one; so to us, it was miraculous, just miraculous. One of the primary differences is that he is beginning to have a sense of himself and his capability that he didn't have before. His self-esteem has improved, and he feels really good about himself.

The last thing I would say is, "talk to others," because when you don't create support, it becomes a very lonely and isolated journey. It's much easier when you create a network around yourself of people having the same conversation.

dr. louis
vismara

When Mark Vismara was born, his parents Dr. Lou and Wendy Vismara looked forward to a picture perfect future for him. Since Mark's autism diagnosis, his parents have done everything in their power to ensure that their son has every opportunity to develop his fullest potential. Lou, inspired by his dedication to his son, made the commitment to help other children and families living with autism. He and three other dads of children with autism mobilized their efforts to help establish what was destined to become The M.I.N.D. Institute at the University of California at Davis.

It's encouraging to see autism begin to receive the support it deserves. It's the beginning…the tip of the iceberg.

I have four children: three daughters, ages 28, 25, and 17, and my son Mark, who is almost 14. When Mark was born, it was an incredibly impactful event. We knew he was going to be a boy. He was beautiful. What was compelling was that he looked exactly like I did when I was a very young child. The first year of his life, he met all of his developmental milestones. We first became concerned with Mark when he was about 13 months old. He was initially doing some babbling and that receded. His language wasn't developing.

I remember waking up one morning, and suddenly the thought came to my mind, "Could Mark be autistic?" What was unusual was that he was an incredibly cuddly child. In retrospect, it was probably more of a tactile sensation of rubbing against the skin than an emotional connection.

When Mark was 20 months old, we had him seen by a developmental psychologist and two developmental pediatricians. Within a couple of weeks, we got the diagnosis that Mark had full blown autism. It was right around the fourth of July—it was one of the worst times of our lives.

I've never told this story before, but I was always picked on and teased when I was a kid. When I was a young child, I came over from Italy; I didn't speak the language, I wore different looking clothes, and the kids would always pick on me. Mark was a handsome and athletic-looking little guy. I remember looking at him and saying, "You're going to have a great life. No one's ever going to pick on you." My expectations were suddenly broken and shattered. I was devastated.

I have to say that we were incredibly fortunate. My wife Wendy and I have a good relationship. We were committed and had economic resources. We had a stable home life.

For the first two years after Mark's diagnosis we were in survival mode. We researched all of the resources. We learned

that 40 hours of ABA was advised, so we had 60. We didn't share it with anyone outside of our immediate family. We had the full gamut of emotions: anger, frustration, guilt and shame. I can remember early on in Mark's diagnosis when we would be in the grocery store, and Mark might be misbehaving. I remember being terribly embarrassed, trying to go down a different aisle so that my patients and friends wouldn't see us. I can remember being terribly jealous of families with typically developing children.

Someone taught me early in my medical school training that time is a wonderful, soothing balm. That certainly has been the case for my family and Mark. The turning point for me was about two-and-a-half years after Mark's diagnosis. We had been living with a bunker mentality, not sharing Mark's diagnosis, leading a very cloistered life. It wasn't working. One day I felt that because of the training that I had in medical school as a cardiologist, I could use some of those skill sets in terms of trying to make a difference not only in Mark's life but in the lives of other children and families who perhaps didn't have the resources.

About ten years ago, some other parents and I decided that we really needed to bring autism to the attention of mainstream medicine. We approached the University of California at Davis about starting a comprehensive research center. Having lived in the California state capital for 35 years, I was privileged to take care of some wonderful individuals. During the period of our greatest need, they stepped up to the plate to help. This was the genesis of The M.I.N.D. Institute, which is making great contributions to our understanding of autism. I really became enthralled with trying to be an agent for change, and for the past seven years, I've been working as a policy consultant at the California State Senate.

The first message that I would share with parents of young children with autism is one of hope. In the 12 years since my son's diagnosis, there have been exponential changes in terms of what we understand about autism—the science behind it, the interventions, and the treatments. It's so encouraging to see autism begin to receive the support it deserves. It's the beginning, the tip of the iceberg.

All of us can live without food for a very long period of time, without shelter, clothing and water. But I have learned that without hope, there really is no essence of a meaningful life. The hopes I have for Mark are no different than the hopes I have for my other three children: that they are and will be good individuals, that they will be the best that they possibly can, and that they will be caring. I hope they love themselves and that their lives will make a difference—that the world will be a better place because they have been here.

It's interesting that autism is characterized by social aloofness, withdrawal and inability to interact. There are times in my relationship with Mark when we share an incredible bond that almost transcends, that borders on spiritual. Can we get together and talk about the Sacramento Kings or how the Los Angeles Dodgers are doing? No, I miss that. There are times, though, when we bond at a very intense level—it's very real. I treasure those times and I keep them in my heart and soul. They are priceless.

elena and walter
cervantes

lena and Walter Cervantes knew that their teenage son
Johnny needed a special environment that would help
him deal with his Asperger's Disorder. Their younger son,
Danny, also has an autism spectrum disorder, although less
severe in nature; their youngest child, Jacqueline, developed
typically. Elena and Walter struggled until they found the
educational opportunity that would enable Johnny to be at
peace with himself and to be happy. Now they are able to say
with smiles on their faces that Johnny's future is looking
very bright.

It was so hard to accept the fact that we had wasted so many years.

Elena: The biggest problem we had is that they kept saying, "Johnny's a very good-looking child; he's so sweet; he's so nice; there's nothing really wrong with him." But when he was in second grade, we started to notice that he was falling behind. There was just something that wasn't right with him. I took him to a doctor who finally spelled it out. It was very hard to accept the fact that we had wasted so many years.

Walter: When we approached the school and told them about it, they said, "Look, he's a perfectly sweet child. Don't put him in a special class; you don't want your neighbors and the people in town to know about it. You don't want to label your child." So I told them, "Don't talk to me like that. What matters is that my child gets an education and that he gets ahead. I couldn't care less about what anyone thinks."

The school encouraged us to take him to a special education class, so I visited the place. I was really disappointed when I saw what was going on, because it was a hodgepodge of children. Disabilities were mixed there, and some of the children could be very, very disturbing for my son. We did send him there for summer session, and one of the children attacked the teacher, biting her. My son said, "Please don't send me there anymore."

So we gave up on that route, and he went back to the regular public school for the third grade. He had a teacher who was so dedicated and very structured, and Johnny loved it because every move, every thing was structured. There were only 20 students in the class, and the teacher could manage quite well. Johnny was very happy; he thrived there. But the following two years were disastrous.

After Christmas, he told us that he didn't want to go back there anymore. Then he told us about the teasing—that they made fun of him, they called him names. He said he wanted to commit suicide if we forced him to go back to school. That's how he ended up hospitalized for two weeks on suicide watch when he was ten years old; he had a nervous breakdown. That was one

of the hardest things we have gone through in our lives. The doctors from UCLA said Johnny can't go back to his school, and they recited all of the reasons why. The school insisted, "Oh, he's fine here. We don't have a special class for him, but we take him aside, and in the teacher's office he'll get his education." So we said, "It's time to get a lawyer," and then they changed their minds and provided funding for a specialized school for Johnny.

By then the family was devastated; it was hard on all of us. Our son Daniel is one year younger than Johnny, and he's also diagnosed autistic. It's so hard because since Johnny was more severe, all of our attention was focused on Johnny. It's unfair but you help the one that needs it the most. And it's very hard for our youngest child, our daughter; she complains all the time saying that we're either with Johnny or Daniel. She says, "What about me? You never think of me." We try to balance, but it's hard.

When Johnny came to his new school, it was in the summer, for only one month. He said, "Please, Daddy, don't take me out. I want to stay here; I'm so happy here." At first he used to call it the non-teasing school. We have come to the realization that the question of what's normal and what isn't is a matter of semantics. He still has problems, but we see a future. School makes him happy, and it makes me happy to see him happy. He really looks forward to coming to school and learning. He just really loves it. How could you not be happy when you finally see your child in a place where he's happy? We're a family, and the family mission is to take care of the children until they're able to take care of themselves.

Elena: We wish we could have done something before, but we are glad that we finally got him here. He's changed completely; he's another child.

Walter: You have to look forward; you just can't dwell on things. I get angry with what happened to Johnny in the beginning. It could have been prevented and we were denied that. It doesn't do me any good zeroing into something that's negative. Now, I look at his happy face. I hear him say that his teacher is wonderful, that he can talk to the boys in his class, and that they won't laugh at him. All his needs are actually taken care of—they not only teach him, but they're very compassionate. The teachers really care for Johnny—more than just scholastic things, they care about the person, and that's a blessing in itself. You have to focus on the positive.

joanne and tom
palmer

The Palmers have three sons. Early on they knew that Carson was developing differently. They found hope for Carson in an intensive early intervention preschool for children with autism spectrum disorders. Joanne and Tom recently renewed their wedding vows on their tenth anniversary and celebrated having weathered the storms of Carson's early development. Joanne now advocates publicly for autism awareness, early identification and intervention.

Early intervention has given our child back to us.

Joanne: At about a year and a half, Carson started having severe wild tantrums. He wouldn't let anyone touch him anymore. He was almost completely out of control. He wouldn't let his brother Kane touch him. He would go to Tom, to me, and to my father, but no other family or friends could get near him. It took more than two years before Carson would go to my best friend at all, and she saw him every single day.

We had a very long session with a therapist at the regional center, probably three or four hours. At the end of that appointment, she told us that Carson has autism, but he's high functioning. When she said "autism," it was like our child was kidnapped. It was like they just took everything away. You don't think, "What do we do *right now*?" You see this big overwhelming picture. Maybe there won't be a future for my child. I might be taking care of this child for the rest of my life. The therapist said, "The outcome for someone like Carson could be very good if you get him into therapy as soon as possible. He needs speech. He needs a lot of one-on-one with people who are trained to deal with kids who are autistic." We also got a couple of private evaluations, and everyone gave us the same answer: "Yes, he's autistic and get help." So that's when we started.

I am definitely a firm believer in early intervention. Honestly, when we think about where Carson was when he started, and where he might be today if he didn't have all the services that he's had over the last couple of years! It was only getting worse just before we enrolled him in the Young Learners Preschool. And if he had not been enrolled and would have continued getting worse, I can't imagine what kind of a child we would have. I don't know what it would've done to our family, to our older son. We probably wouldn't have had Cooper, our third child, because we would've been too afraid. Early intervention has given our child back to us, a child who's happy and has a great future.

When he started in Young Learners, we'd ask him every day, "Carson, what did you do today?" and he would never tell us. Instead, we would get this: "Godzilla, Godzilla and dinosaurs." So the only way I knew what was happening was by email with

the teacher or the daily reports sent home through the journal. She would tell me everything that he had done, but he would never say anything. I kept asking, "When is he going to tell us just one thing that he's done?" Finally one day, my husband was sitting quietly next to him and getting ready to read a book before bed, and Carson looks up at Tom and all of a sudden says, "Daddy, Daddy, say, "Carson how was school today?" Tom responded, "Carson, how was school today?" and came out of the room with tears in his eyes. That's when we knew we'd broken through into this kind of social circle, that he was going to start having conversations with us.

From that day on, every single night, Tom couldn't wait to get in there and say, "Carson, how was school today?" At first he might just tell us one thing: "We painted today," or "I had speech today." Then he'd go into Godzilla and lizards and talk about various bugs and creatures. But it's been a couple of months since that time, and now he comes home saying, "Daddy, look at my art project. And Momma, look, I did a pumpkin today. Momma, I played with Charles today. And there's a new student in the classroom." Now we get several explanations of things that he's done, and that's huge because we never thought it would happen.

Tom: You saw him light up when he realized, "Wow, I'm communicating with my mom and dad now." I've made this connection, whether it's a word or an emotion or even if it's angry or sad, when he saw that we could understand what he was communicating to us and that we would respond to him, the frustration level and the anger and the tantrums started to go away.

When he was finally able to do that, we felt like we had the child back that we had lost. Now, instead of worrying about what's going to happen, we're totally confident that Carson's going to have a normal future. When he was younger and couldn't have these conversations with us, we wondered and worried. Now we have our child back; we can do anything and go anywhere. There's a magic about Carson that comes out when he discovers something or he finds a new word. He beams when he's happy; there's a discovery there.

There's all this mystery about autism. Are there parts of his brain that aren't developing? What parts maybe are developing

at a more rapid rate? What's locked inside there? I'm so excited to find out what he's going to be interested in. Right now he's interested in everything, all the things that little boys are, but what's going to be his special thing? That's the kind of a wonderful journey we're on with him, and that's the way we've looked at it all along. We'll just support him in the best way we can, make sure he's got everything he needs, all the love, all the therapy, so he can communicate and be a happy person. It's all about making sure he has joy in his life, and in the end that becomes this kind of magic for us—what's he going to become, what's he going to do.

deborah
fils

It took eight years for Deborah and Elliott Fils' son Gregory to be diagnosed with high functioning autism. From the beginning, they knew Gregory was not developing typically like his older sister, Andrea, did. Even without a diagnosis, the Fils gave him a full range of educational and therapeutic opportunities. As they look back, they are very grateful that they took this path.

...there has to be a place for everyone.

For eight years, every specialist we spoke to said, "Well, we don't know what he has, but he definitely does not have autism." So until Gregory was ten and a half, he did not have a diagnosis of autism. He would gesture the best he could; he would push you to places where he wanted you to go; and he had very pragmatically appropriate, almost non-verbal communication. He would sit there and take turns nodding his head, with nonsense sounds, almost trying to converse; so everyone was convinced he was not autistic, because he craved social interaction. But as time went on, some of his perseverative tendencies and lack of social graces became more prominent; and I think the spectrum widened during that time and there became a place available for him on the autistic spectrum.

Even though he didn't have a label of autism, the only comfort we had in taking eight years to get that label was that we had done everything right. We were in occupational therapy for all those years, and we had physical therapy, speech therapy, and social skills therapy. We did everything that you do with a child on the autistic spectrum. We tapped into all of those resources. So at least in hindsight we didn't kick ourselves for missing out on helpful interventions.

My husband Elliott and I had different "worst fears" for Gregory. Mine was autism. Elliott was not as crushed by the diagnosis as I was. Fortunately, it wasn't a big surprise, and Gregory's disabilities were not a big surprise. We had seen them for so many years prior to having a name put on it, but we both still deal with it in different ways. It will surface on different occasions.

For example, one time we were planning something for Gregory, and Elliott asked, "Did you tell this person that we're going to hire that Gregory has special needs?" And I answered, "No, I don't think we need to. We can do that later down the line." But Elliott said, "I think we need to do it now to make sure that he can handle it and he can accommodate everything."

So it just seems more important or more significant to each of us in different areas at different times. I can see how we've remained strong through it, but I can also see how families really

can break apart from this extra stress. It's not what you sign up for when you get married, when you plan to have children. Fortunately, it hasn't done that to us. It's made us stronger, but it's really not what you expect.

Before his recent placement in a school designed specifically to meet his needs, Gregory wasn't successful in the other school environments. He was getting angrier and the teacher's assistant would say things like, "He doesn't respect me," and we would explain to her, "It's not that he doesn't respect you. He has special needs, and his social skills are not that of a typical nine-year-old. You know, if he were able to perform a certain way, he wouldn't have special needs." Gregory locks horns very easily. If you discipline him too hard, he will get angry and back off and not be productive at all.

When he had his first bad day in his new school, one of the administrators called and said, "Gregory's new to us. You need to let us know what works best for him." So I told them, "If you tell him what needs to be done and back off, within several seconds he'll probably come around and do what's expected of him." So the next time he had a bad day, they tried that and it worked. It doesn't always work; at times he will still lock horns and be completely unproductive.

In the other school environment, no-one really listened to us. No one would change his or her response, so as to not let him win in any way; but perhaps just having a social exchange with him in a different manner would have helped to increase his productivity.

He doesn't know about the diagnostic label that he has. He'll sometimes say that words are hard for him to say, so he knows that some things are more difficult. He knows he takes medicine to help control his behavior, and sometimes he'll say, "My body's telling me to be angry, my body's telling me to do something bad," and so he'll know he's struggling—he'll know. And I see him having these battles within himself and it's heartbreaking. Life is very difficult for him, but we tell him, "We'll help you," and sometimes give him a big hug. I think that's emotional support, but also sometimes I really think it's a sensory input issue for him. So sometimes we'll just give him a big tight squeeze and say, "Come on, we'll help you," and that helps calm him down, to know that we're not going to get angry when he has these struggles within himself.

He knows that life is hard for him. We try to remind him that parts of life are hard for other people too. He does know of some extra challenges that he has. As parents we learned to find, acknowledge, and enjoy his strengths. And that's what's given us strength. Everybody has something. Not everything is visible, not all of it is public, but everybody has something, and there has to be a place for everyone.

sharon
emanuelli

Sharon Emanuelli and her husband, Michael Kaiser, have seen at first hand how compelling their teenage son Sandro's challenges with Asperger's can be. Although Sandro is intellectually gifted, his problems with social interaction and the interpretation of everyday situations often made his experiences negative and isolating. He needed to be taught the social skills that most of us take for granted.

Sandro is difficult to pin down—he doesn't fit any classic group of symptoms...

I was looking for an arts-oriented school, because Sandro had already shown me that he was very good at writing stories, and he did a lot of artwork. He made a little cartoon video when he was five, just out of his own head. I pushed the button on the camera, but he did all the work for it and understood how things could be animated. He was also very musical and wanted to play the violin. I wanted an arts situation. We were applying to private schools and nobody would take him; they said he took too much attention away from the other kids. So he spent his kindergarten year at his preschool, which had a very nice kindergarten. When we had to move, his new school said that we needed to get a psychologist to work with us and then they would be happy to have him. And so that's when we first had him tested, at age six.

The psychologist we worked with was very well-meaning, but he wasn't looking to give him a diagnosis. And I think he didn't really want to give him a diagnosis. We would hear, "He's a little unusual, but not that unusual." And it seemed like it could be slightly age inappropriate or just a little immature. And as he got older, those things that should have developed never did. His elementary school had a very definite approach to discipline, which worked for a lot of kids, but it wasn't always working for him. And the teachers refused to do things—like a lot of positive reinforcement—because they didn't want to "addict" him to that. But he had no motivation to behave the way they wanted him to, because he didn't understand why it was more appropriate; and he needed positive reinforcement, a lot of it, in order to manage. It wasn't until the end of fifth grade that I insisted on getting him tested again.

His learning disability had to do with not being able to function in a social situation without being told what to do. I remember an incident at the beginning of second grade, a year after he'd started at this particular school, which had all-school meetings on Friday mornings. All the kids would sit around in this ordered circle and perform for each other. They sang songs,

talked about what they'd done during the week, and gave little reports. The parents could come and it was just a very nice situation. Sandro was always getting in trouble for talking or moving around, and finally I said to him, "Sandro, you have to be quiet in all-school meetings. You have to pay attention and be quiet." And he burst into tears and said, "Why didn't anyone tell me?" He needed more than a cue. He needed to be told straight out, this is what you do and this is why you do it. He may still have had difficulty managing his impulses on occasion, but after that it was easier for him.

The testing doctor said he has some traits of Asperger's. Sandro is difficult to pin down, because he doesn't fit any classic group of symptoms that would allow you to say definitively that he has Asperger's. But he does have Asperger's in my mind. That's how I can deal with understanding how he thinks; why his logic—his social logic—is so different; why he doesn't understand that if he's angry at someone, he can't lash out at anybody else. Or, if he's angry at his teacher, he can't start hitting the kid next to him. He was more often verbally aggressive, just yelling. He never really hurt anybody. When he got angry, he did things that would let the kid know that he was angry, but the other kid might have done nothing wrong.

I gave Sandro a book to read, *Freaks, Geeks, and Asperger's Syndrome*, by another 13—year-old-boy who was quite delightful. And at first that made Sandro pick out all of his eccentric mannerisms and exaggerate them for fun, thinking that was great. But then after that, I just said, "You know, look, that's not really the way to take this. You need to realize that you need to do certain things and be certain ways when you're around other people." I remind him, I try to point out when he's doing things that aren't appropriate. I explain, "This is why you do this, but you need to understand that other people don't see it the same way. They have a different way of looking at things, and if you try to see it the way other people do, then you'll understand better and maybe not do things that get you in trouble." He doesn't feel good about himself, either, when those things happen.

I guess I would like people to understand that when a child has such difficulty, it's not because they are bad kids. They may do things that seem bad. The behavior is bad. But they may not understand how to change it, or why it's even necessary to change it. They're coping with the input that they get.

He's a very creative kid. I hope that he'll find something that he likes doing. I hope he will have a family. I hope he will work and be self-sufficient, and I can foresee that he will be. But maybe not as soon as some other people.

mary and bill
urquhart

B ill and Mary Urquhart have three children, Christine, Brian and Abigail. When Brian's early development came to an abrupt halt at about 18 months of age, his parents, Mary and Bill, began an uphill journey. They refused to accept the dismal prognosis that they were given and vigorously pursued education and therapy for Brian. As they look back over the past decade, they celebrate all of the strides that Brian has made that others thought wouldn't be possible.

Now he has some real friends, which is pretty amazing.

Mary: We called Brian "Lumpo Man." That was his nickname because he really didn't have many expressions, and he wasn't very lively. I breastfed Brian, but he never would lay very close to me. Then one night I remember he had stomach cramps, and he just laid against me for the first time. It's such a vivid recollection because I thought, "My God, he has never lain against me." He was always so tense, but we really didn't know anything was wrong.

Bill: Brian seemed to be developing relatively normally up until he was maybe about a year or a little bit over a year; because he was speaking words, and all of a sudden it seemed like he just withdrew into himself and stopped communicating to the point where, frankly, I thought he was deaf.

Mary: And the doctors thought he was deaf, and I kept taking him to have hearing tests. And they'd say, "Well, you're just not accepting that your son is deaf," and I said, *"He is not deaf."*

Bill: Finally, we found out that his brain was receiving sounds normally, but he was just completely withdrawn. So, Mary met with an evaluation team from the school district.

Mary: They were very lovely. They came and met with me and said they'd like to see Brian in this play group for children who were 18 months old. When I took him, all the other children would sit with their mothers in the play group; and I would try to hold Brian down, and then I'd get up and tackle him as he was running toward the street, and I was just a mess. I just didn't know what to do. They said, "Well, we think he's autistic."

I remember seeing the car, and I actually had a cast on my ankle from playing tennis. I had my son in my arms and I thought, "I can make it to the car," short of breath, "I can make it, I can make it." I got him in the car and I started crying and I called Bill.

Bill: We went to see a specialist who, basically, said, "There's no hope for your child, he's going to be institutionalized by the time he's 12." My wife is not somebody who gives up at anything. Mary had a thriving consulting business, and she just gave it up and then made the improvement of Brian her vocation.

Fortunately, we became associated with some other parents who got together with a local special education school, and formed a school for young kids who had autism. The only people you want to speak to are other parents because what happens is, everybody's well meaning. Everybody feels your pain, or at least they think they feel your pain, but they don't really know what your pain is. They'll tell you, "Oh, this will get better; he seems like such a cute boy." You know that's not going to happen, and the only ones that you can talk to honestly are the other parents.

Mary: Brian was in the special schools until he was six, and then we mainstreamed him. So for a few years he was in a full inclusion classroom. When we placed him in a specialized school at 14, they said, "We're a school full of children with autism. And he needs to know that he has autism; it's time." So it was very hard for Brian, because he really thought he was better than everyone else. He didn't know he was autistic. If you asked him to describe himself, he'd say, "I'm a genius," or, "I'm an amazing artist."

For about four months, it was very hard for him to understand that not only wasn't he better than everyone else, but he had some things that were worse and perceived to be worse. The school tries to help the students take the things that they have and improve them and work with them. But what has helped is that he's met a number of children and he has some relationships, he has some friends. The interactions that he's had there have been amazing.

He had friends come over before, but they came over because we said, "We'll take you to Disneyland if you go with Brian," and they kind of came along for the ride—lovely, lovely kids, just wonderful. But, now he has some real friends, which is pretty amazing, it's incredible.

Bill: We did a pretty darn good job of helping him steer a path academically. But we were kind of clueless about how to get him to interact socially in ways I guess that the rest of society thinks are more appropriate. And it seems like he's just grown so much as a human being since he came to this school.

Mary: At first we could only think one week at a time, and then when we could think about his future one month ahead of where we were, that was really great. And now we're thinking a year ahead. He is doing so well.

karen shapiro and
syud sharif

K aren Shapiro and her husband Syud Sharif have two sons, David and Benjamin, who are four years apart in age. Based on their experience with their older son Benjamin, they began to sense that David was developing differently. As difficult as the diagnosis is to accept, they want other parents to know that it is very important to seek intervention as soon as possible.

You have to take risks and go in the direction that is right.

Karen: I don't think I went through denial. It's not that I didn't say: "What did I do wrong? Did I eat something wrong? Did I do something in my pregnancy? Maybe I shouldn't have given him a shot. How did this happen?" But in life, my attitude is, we need to work with what we have and to look back and grow from it. If this doctor we trusted (who was highly recommended), if the psychologist we were seeing, and if his teacher were all saying something is going on here, we need to have respect for David and forget about what's going on inside us.

It's my personality, and I think ours, to look at the positive in a situation, but that doesn't mean that I wanted my child to be autistic. I certainly don't want any child to have to face that. But if that's what's there, then I have to deal with it. I need to do what's best for my child—and that was to take action very quickly.

When we first got the diagnosis, I knew that the first three years were going to be very critical. We had known enough to realize that by the time they're six or seven, there's a wiring that is already in place. But if we could reach him early, I knew that he would shine, he would come out. He would always be an autistic child, but he could get on the higher end. We could get him communicating. We could get him to be everything he could possibly be.

You have to take risks and go in the direction you think is right. You learn as you go: what fits, what doesn't fit; what works, what doesn't work.

Syud: The other thing we did was we got our oldest son Benjamin involved, which I think was the smartest thing to do because it was really hard on him. Benjamin was all of a sudden neglected, and our focus was entirely on David. We realized very quickly that we cannot neglect Benjamin, and we sat down and talked to him about the issues David was facing, and how he could be a part of it, how he could help David.

David would never hit any child in school or any other social setting. But he would lash out at home. He lashed out because

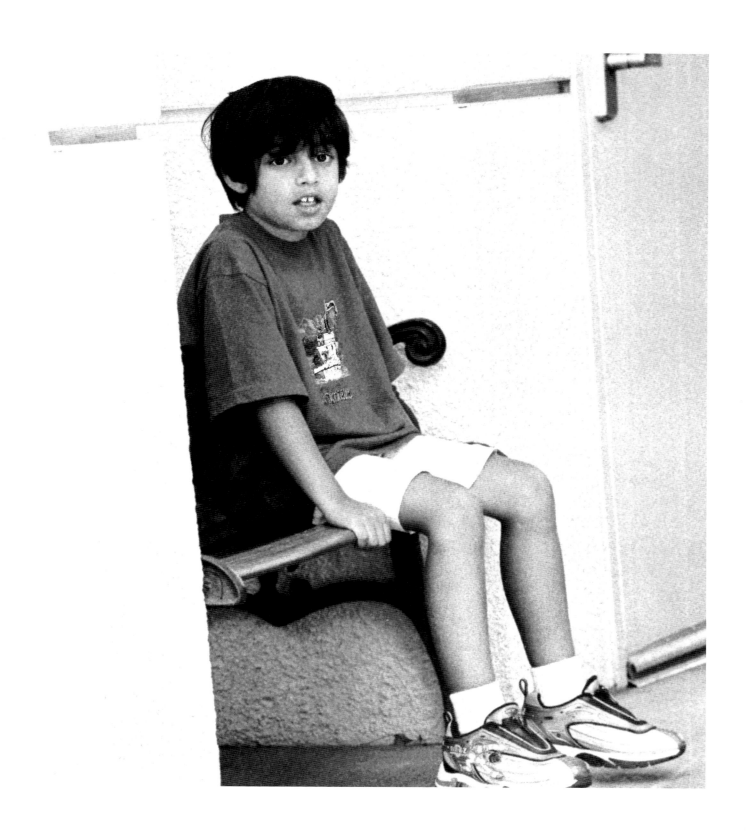

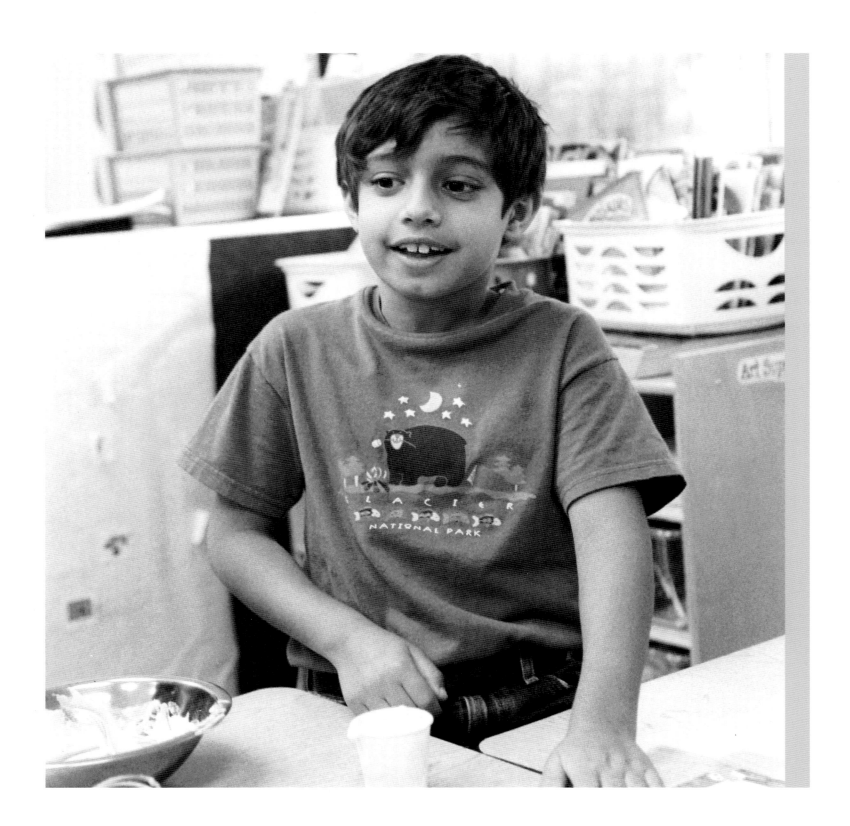

he was unable to express himself and communicate what he wanted or what he was feeling. Benjamin would get the brunt of it, and he is such a sweetheart, such an accommodating child. He would bend over backwards to do anything for David. But there came a point when we had to tell Benjamin to draw some lines and be a little firm. While it's wonderful to be giving and caring, you can't let David run all over you.

Karen: You have to take the risks and go in the direction you think is right and learn as you go: what fits, what doesn't fit; what works, what doesn't work. If you just deny it, you don't give your child the opportunity to have everything that child can have. And the older the child gets, the harder it is for that child.

I think that if my child is labeled as autistic, so be it. He can do what he can do to the best of his abilities. It's not the label that matters. We are not paralyzed by the stigma of autism.

I feel very proud that he is successful, that he is doing theater. He did a production of "Free to Be You and Me" with a group of regular kids. He also did a production of "Charlie and the Chocolate Factory." He loves his dance class, he loves piano, and he loves to perform. I knew if we could find those things that light a spark in him and inspire him, we could really do a lot for him; and I feel like we have. There's more to do, but I feel really good that we took action as soon as when we found out.

I don't wish this on any parent, but I can say that I've learned to be a better Mom to both my kids from this experience. I've learned about sensory issues—including my own—because I had to deal with David's sensory issues, of not letting anyone cut or comb his hair, or touch or kiss him. I didn't understand why he didn't like to be kissed. And now I see how it's in all of us to varying degrees. With him it's a little bit more that way. He doesn't get the back-and-forth aspect, that there's another person there who has feelings. But he's still a loving child who has a lot to bring.

Syud: If you succumb to fear of labels, do you really do justice to your child? You cannot provide him or her with the opportunities to blossom and grow to their fullest potential if you're afraid that your efforts will be dashed by the stigma. We both feel strongly that to help a child reach his or her potential, that's what life is all about.

cheryl
green

Cheryl Green is a deeply religious woman who believes that her daughter, Irene, came into to her life for a higher purpose—to help Cheryl see the beauty in everyone and everything around her, to help her to become a stronger person and to become an advocate for children in need. Cheryl feels that Irene's beauty and contentment bring joy to all of the people who come to know her.

Irene always brings me back to what's important in the world…

By her first birthday there was obviously a need to go to a doctor and discover why I had a 12-month-old child who couldn't say "mama." I'm a very talkative person, my mom's a very talkative person, and I knew a child who came from my womb by 12 months would be most likely an early talker! That's when I sensed it was time to talk with a pediatrician and express some concerns.

I also made a note that during her regular pediatrician appointment that I would mention that Irene has not transitioned to solid foods and doesn't say "mommy," which doesn't seem natural. So I mentioned this to the pediatrician, and, at that point, she reassured me that all children develop differently and that there was no sign of anything. In my spirit I didn't agree, but what can you say.

I went out to lunch with a girlfriend, who is an occupational therapist, and as I began to prepare Irene's oatmeal there in the restaurant, my friend says to me, "Cheryl, why is Irene, who is 12 months old, still eating oatmeal?" I explained that she was not eating solid foods, or finger foods or anything like that. She was very firm with me, and said I should have Irene checked out because she should be chewing and eating different foods. I knew that what she was telling me was something that she understood and experienced in a professional way. My friend sent me a stack of information on autism. She got it already, but it was hard for her to break it to me. It began to register with me that the information she was sharing was certainly in line with what I knew about Irene as her mom. I had never gotten that information from the doctors. The pediatricians had never made mention of this possibility. When I finally got the diagnosis, I was just crushed. The saddest part is that they tell you and you have all these questions. They don't have a cure, they don't have answers.

Once I got her to a preschool for children with autism, I discovered that my child had been playing me like a fiddle: she had the capability to feed herself, but as long as she had a

mommy who didn't know any better, she was playing me. So the greatest benefit that I got from this program is that it revealed all these capabilities. Irene had these self-help skills that she never got to use at home. Her teachers had to set me straight, and say, "Irene can put on her own socks; Irene can feed herself." I was babying her, limiting what should be expected of her, because I just didn't know she had the ability.

When I saw how well she was respecting the teachers and being such a big girl, at home I had a brand new program for her. I put together the exact same schedule: "Brush your teeth, Irene," and she looked at me as if to say, "How did you figure that out?" At home it's a whole new routine.

I would just like to encourage all parents—if you think there's a chance that your child could possibly have some developmental delays, to get them diagnosed early and get them involved in early intervention as early as possible. Take your child to everything that is offered so they can become more functional, to excel and to overcome autism.

Irene is such a special little ball of energy. She'll be five years old next month; she's really wonderful. God has done everything I prayed for. She was non-verbal for a very long time, and now she certainly has language skills, and I've even found myself saying, "Irene, be quiet!" She has a precious little pitch in her voice, like a beautiful little voice, and she's just very energetic. She has so much joy. She doesn't seem aware of her autism or her differences, and she's just always full of joy. Irene always brings me back to what's important in the world, because she seems very, very clear on things that all of us can learn from. She's just always in the now.

ellen and kirk
hartman

Ellen and Kirk Hartman have three daughters: Harriet, Gina and Julie. Unlike her sisters who developed typically, Gina has autism. Ellen and Kirk are open and honest about Gina's challenges and have dedicated themselves to ensuring that Gina has every chance to succeed. They have always made living a life as a happy family a top priority.

I want my kids to look back and say that we were a happy family…

Ellen: There's nothing you want less than this kind of diagnosis for your child. However, I couldn't get any help for Gina until I had a diagnosis. I stated my concerns to my pediatrician and I tried to get some speech therapy, physical therapy and occupational therapy. And we were somewhat successful in getting services. But the main problem was that no one believed that Gina was autistic. I spoke to friends and relatives—and eventually even took her to a pediatric neurologist—and they were all dismissive. They said that Gina was born so prematurely (two months early) that I needed to let her catch up. Even though I knew it was more than that, my hands were tied until I had a diagnosis.

Kirk: You have to be an advocate for your child. It is the hardest thing to do, to always be there for your child, whether it's with school districts, services that are out there, or insurance. It's emotionally draining at the end of a long day, but you can't be shy about doing it.

Ellen: We've always been open about Gina's diagnosis. We've never hidden the fact that we have an autistic child, and frankly, even if we had wanted to hide it—which we never did—we couldn't, because now that Gina's older, she's out in the community. When she is out in the community, she always has an adult with her and some of her behaviors are somewhat peculiar.

Kirk: I think it's important that these children are a part of the community. Everyone in the town where we live knows who Gina is, and they're all incredibly nice to her; she's part of the fabric.

Ellen: Now Gina is 13. She can't sit at home and do a puzzle all day. So she does go out. I will write a supermarket list and give it to her companion, and they will go and find the things on my list and bring them to the front and wait in line and, if possible, handle the exchange of money. Sometimes that's too much for

her, but other times, she can do simple money transactions and count the change. For Gina to learn things that are functional is really our focus now. When you have a child like this, your first priority as a parent is that they're safe, and you also want them to be successful.

Kirk: You don't want them too frustrated, and the frustration factor can build up very quickly. That's something that you've got to guard against by finding a program that is appropriate, where the curriculum is tailored to your child's needs and abilities. Also, being out in the community helps Gina feel some independence and feel good about herself. And she enjoys it.

Ellen: The goal is to make your child be as independent as possible. And you want to raise your child's level of functioning, but all within in the parameters of your child being safe and understanding what's appropriate. I remember being in a park years ago and a girl who had some kind of developmental disability, possibly autism, came running up and gave me a huge hug. I was looking around to find out who was in charge of this little girl, which was not immediately apparent to me. I said to her, "You don't know me well enough to be hugging me." That behavior is an obvious concern because some of these kids really don't know who gets a close hug and who gets a far-away hug, who just gets a handshake and who gets a wave, and who gets nothing.

I remember when we were given the diagnosis and told that Gina's not going to have the life that we thought. Our older daughter Harriet was three and we hadn't yet had our youngest daughter, Julie. Even though I knew it—deep down—there was something so final about getting the diagnosis and I was stunned and grief-stricken for quite a while. Eventually I snapped out of my funk one day when a friend said, "Gina won't have the life you thought she would have—and neither will Harriet." That made me angry because I thought, "You watch and see what kinds of lives these girls are going to have." I realized I owed them the opportunity to have the best lives that they could possibly have. It truly was that one comment that day that made me realize that life had to go on and it had to be good.

Just make sure that everybody lives a good life in your family, including you. I feel everybody is entitled to joy in their life. And it may not even seem possible when you're first getting a diagnosis of autism, but it is. Trust your instincts; even though it may not be something you want to hear, that drum is going to keep beating louder and louder and you're going to have to hear it sooner or later. Make sure there's joy in your life.

Kirk: We go out every Saturday night. I think it is important that you have a life. I think it is important that your children see you enjoying your life and enjoying each other. So, you can't lose sight of the fact that it's important to have fun.

Ellen: I want my kids to look back and say that we were a happy family that we had fun and we do.

love

■ Andrews ■ Mantegna ■ Paul & Canby
■ Reyes ■ Maldonado ■ Martin
■ Schneider ■ Spalding
■ Almog ■ Wade

The parents I have met are remarkable people—heroic in their efforts on behalf of their children—it is the heroism that is born of love and sustained by love. They have stayed the course—their love is unconditional and long lasting. Their insights are inspiring and speak to the very essence of what it means to truly love.

When Joe Mantegna's daughter Mia was born, she was three months premature and weighed only 1 lb. 12 ozs. When he was first introduced to Mia, he remembers donning scrubs and that the nurses supported him under each of his arms. He didn't understand why, until he met Mia. The sign on the incubator read "Baby Mantegna." Joe saw that sign, looked at his daughter, and was overtaken with a profound feeling of love. As his knees buckled beneath him, he understood why the nurses were there. Although he could not foresee that Mia would have autism, he knew that he and his wife, Arlene, and Baby Mantegna would have to "dodge many bullets" together. At that very moment, Joe knew that their love would carry them through.

Like Joe, when parents first welcome a child into their lives they describe their feelings of love as instantaneous. Their feelings become even more intensified when their child begins to return their love with attention and affection. Many parents of children with autism do not have the benefit of this feedback—they may feel that their love is unrequited when their child's gaze doesn't meet theirs, when a hug is rebuffed, passively received, or doesn't quiet an upset child, and smiles aren't shared—yet their love endures.

Love anchors parents as they seek and grapple with the diagnosis and cope with the roller coaster of emotions. It gives them the impetus to move forward as they weather the challenges and the uncertainty. They set aside initial dreams, renew and replenish hope, and manage the trials that each day brings. Love helps parents deal with the stresses on the family dynamic and constraints in the community that they never anticipated when they signed on to have children. There are financial sacrifices that some parents bear in funding services for their children. Some parents give up their careers to devote 24 hours each day to their child. Others do not have that option, others are single parents, and scramble to put together viable care options. Parents search for the education and treatment for their child which can necessitate uprooting an entire family or separating the family. They face the decision whether or not to have more children. They try to find ways to give their other children the time and attention that they deserve and to help them understand why the rules may be different for their brother or sister with autism. Although some find that their extended families can be counted on to offer them support and encouragement, others don't have the benefit of this support. Friends can be very supportive or they can shy away, not wanting or knowing how to deal with the situation or wanting to be involved.

Having a child with autism doesn't give a family a free pass from all of the life stressors. Some couples have told me that the stress on the marital relationship can contribute to the dissolution of marriage. For others, there is the intensification of their relationship, although it is a changed relationship course together. Joanne and Tom Palmer told me that they recently renewed their vows on the occasion of their tenth anniversary—they said it was a celebration of their ability to stay together given the added challenges of their child's autism.

But through it all, I have had so many parents tell me that all they had to do and endure for the sake of their children was worth it. They say that just when they were sure that their well was dry and that they were losing the battle, they found that they had still more reserve.

The love that children with autism feel for their families may take forms that our eyes are unable to see. Parents learn that love is communicated in many different ways with different code. The feelings the child with autism has for his family may not be readily apparent to those who look for the eye contact, smiles and the hugs to reveal love. Assumptions are made that conventional expressions of love are the only expressions of love. Recently, I saw one of our students with full autism spectrum with limited verbal skills walk with his teacher to greet his dad who had just arrived on campus. His eyes grew big when he saw his dad. He picked up his pace and nestled awkwardly against his dad—his way of saying, "Hello, I'm so happy that you're here, I love you." Simultaneously, his Dad's eyes welled up with tears.

Ultimately, for many parents love empowers their acceptance of a different reality for their child, different from the story that they would have written when they met their child for the first time. Suzanne Reyes shares, "If I were talking to a parent of an autistic child who had just gotten the diagnosis, I would want them to know that they will find their place, and that they will find peace with it—in their own way. The most important thing for them is just to focus on their child and focus on their family and keep it strong and just love their child."

Parents learn to love their children in a way that they say teaches many important lessons. In accepting their children's differences they have told me that they discover many insights about themselves and learn some of the most important lessons in life. Their love and acceptance enable them to see through and beyond the disability into their child's very essence and being. Some say that although they accept their child for who he is, they still have a yearning for their child to one day recover or be cured. Others say that their children are who they are and they wouldn't change them for anything in this world unless they could be sure that it would make them happier.

All of the stories of the parents whom I have met are love stories.

anna
andrews

The love that Anna Andrews feels for her daughter, Cyntrea, has always been profound. The magnitude of Cyntrea's autism led Anna to make major life-altering decisions. The changes that she undertook to help her daughter tested Anna to the very core of her being. Anna's love for Cyntrea gave her the strength to face each new day.

I felt like my heart was torn out of my body.

I felt like it was just me and Cyntrea. I kept saying, "I'm not going to give up on her." I would never give up on Cyntrea. So I would just try different things to keep me calm. I would call around, search the Internet, and contact Oprah and say, "Please help me. Something is going on with my daughter. I don't know what is, but I know I love her, and I'm not going to give up on her."

My husband and I divorced and I moved to Los Angeles where my sister lived. I thought I could get help for my daughter there, but I was totally disappointed. Cyntrea was placed in a class where they didn't have any clue what was going on—the first day I walked to my car and cried. I left Cyntrea in a classroom with about 15 kids with different disabilities. And the teacher asked me, "What is autism?" So I went to the regional center for services. During this time, Cyntrea was in and out of hospital because of behavioral problems.

Because Cyntrea is severely autistic with severe speech delay, if somebody is bothering her, she has no way to tell me or anyone. She was slamming things, self-injuring, hitting me, and putting holes in the wall. I'm in an apartment and I was going to be evicted. She was getting physically stronger and her behavior was explosive. And she didn't have any safety mechanisms. If you told Cyntrea, "Go upstairs and jump off a building," she would. She doesn't know what a car is; she doesn't know what strangers are. One night when we were coming out of the garage, Cyntrea dashed into the traffic. She was running to the main street and there was no way for me to catch her. I just screamed, and this guy who was an angel, heaven-sent, lifted her up and brought her into the house. I thought, "Okay, this is a wake-up call. I don't want her to hurt herself or me." It was just a safety thing. That's when she started taking medication, with the first admission at UCLA.

My mom even said, "You know, Anna Maria, this is killing you. You're by yourself, Cyrelle [Cyntrea's sister] is going to college, and you can't do this anymore." So I was in denial—this is my baby, I'm going to protect her, and no one else can take care of her like I can. It took me a long time to make the decision to

place her in a residential program. When I did make it, I had a nervous breakdown. I was on medical leave for 30 days, because I felt like my heart was torn out of my body.

I finally told myself that I had to get stronger so I could help her. How can I help Cyntrea? I placed her in a residential program. It's a long-term respite. I haven't signed her over to the state. I'm still her parent, but I needed that help. Every time I wake up, I think about Cyntrea and about my other daughter; they're my driving force. I have no option but to work hard and make a better life for them.

If something happened to me, what would happen to Cyntrea? So I have to explain to my older daughter that once I leave, she has to step in; she has to help Cyntrea because she can't help herself. And Cyrelle understands that completely.

If you have to stand up and scream, do it. You have to be an advocate for your child, because no one else will be. You can't sit and say, "My psychiatrist will help me, my pediatrician will help me, or the regional center in the area will help me." You have to educate yourself about your rights, and learn about policies that impact your child's life, and find out what's going on in your child's school. Find a way to communicate your child's needs, and *don't* take no for an answer.

I felt fear and hopelessness sometimes, definitely fatigue, but mostly fear—fear of the unknown. There are child development charts, but you realize that when your child has autism there is no chart to look at because every child is different.

But there's hope. When I look at Cyntrea now, she's giving me eye contact. For several years, Cyntrea had no eye contact, but now she gives me eye contact and hugs me and says "Mommy." That means the world to me. It's magical. It makes me feel so good inside and it feels like the fight that you've been up against and everything you gave up is worth it. Cyntrea is in an excellent place right now. The residential place she's in is an excellent school, and I thank God for it, I really do. There's always hope: don't give up, don't give up.

joe
mantegna

Actor Joe Mantegna and his wife Arlene have two teenage daughters, Mia and her younger sister, Gina. As a public figure, Joe speaks openly about Mia's high functioning autism and about the love he feels for both of his daughters. He actively spreads the important message that there is help and hope for children with autism spectrum disorders.

The first time I heard the word autism, it hit me like a hammer.

Mia was born very premature. She survived and dodged a million kinds of bullets that affect premature babies. The first time I heard that word autism, it just hit me like a hammer. As much as we wanted to deny it initially, I think we knew in our hearts that we couldn't dodge this last bullet.

There are probably a few billion people on this planet who wouldn't mind changing places with me. "Oh, Joe Mantegna, he's an actor in Hollywood, California. He's very successful. He lives in a big house. I'd trade places with him." But nobody gets a free ride. I didn't get a free ride. On the other hand, would I give all this up if I could take away my daughter's autism? Of course I would—in a heartbeat. But I can't, and it's okay.

Having a child with autism is difficult for a family, but it's the only family we know. Her sister doesn't know what its like not to have a sibling with autism and if that's the worst that happens to all of us in our lifetime, I'll take it.

When my wife was pregnant with our second child I remember thinking to myself—and feeling guilty about it—that this other human being was going to be born and how could I ever love another child more than I love—or as much as I love— Mia. She is the light of my life, and I just felt there's no way that there could be another person who could equal that. But it's so true, that in the second that child was born, it's almost instinctive, there was total love and acceptance. It's not exactly the same, it's equal but different.

We had just gotten the diagnosis for Mia, that she had autism, when we brought Gina home from the hospital for the first time. Mia was at that stage of her autism where if things frightened her, irritated her, like loud sounds, she'd hold her ears, and she would scream. It was a behavior that finally subsided. But at that point, it was very difficult. So that first night in the apartment, the baby's crying and you can't even explain to Mia that this is her sister. So Mia's hysterical, and my wife was so upset and saying, "Oh my God, what're we going to do?"

And I remember looking at her and saying, "Honey, Gina's staying. She's not going anywhere. Whatever we're gonna do, we're gonna have to do it together." And, of course, we looked at each other and laughed.

Gina is one of those special individuals who, because of growing up in a household with a sibling who has special needs, has become a much more complete human being.

Once Mia was mainstreamed in regular classes, teachers, who at the beginning of the year were tentative, never failed to say to us, "We hope your daughter has benefited from being in our class as much as the children and staff have." This made me realize that the world should be a place where we can ultimately integrate kids with differences into society.

I think the important thing is to try to acknowledge your child's autism as early as you can and deal with it as early as you can. I think the biggest mistake parents can make is to let their feelings of remorse and denial stop them from taking action.

I've had people call me or write me to thank me for sharing my experience with autism. They say it has helped them feel more comfortable talking about it and its helped change their

life. Getting a few of those letters makes me absolutely realize that sharing my experiences with the public was the right thing to do.

I tell other parents that once you know your child has autism, get out there and get whatever support, education, or help that's available. Don't let denial stop you—jump in. The more input early on—the more benefits later, so take advantage of all that you can now. Things are much better now than they were in the past.

It's about hope, it's about love, it's about commitment, it's about family—the pebbles in the pool that start the ripples. Start as many ripples as you can.

cathy paul and
nathan canby

Cathy Paul and Nathan Canby love their children Oliver and Nora completely and unconditionally. By the time Oliver was 18 months old, they knew that his behavior was not typical of children his age. It took some time until the diagnosis was made that would provide a roadmap to Oliver's future. They accept his differences and celebrate his loving and caring manner that transcends his Asperger's Disorder.

When we finally got the diagnosis it was the beginning of the good stuff.

Cathy: When Oliver was 18 months old, he memorized all the letters and the numbers and would go up to license plates and read them. The first thing we noticed was that his intelligence and his memory were extraordinary. He had little quirks, like he wouldn't get down to touch the snow. He had certain anxieties. He felt everything more extremely than other kids. But he was still our loving kid. I knew about autism, and once in a while it would cross my mind, but I had no idea that autism encompassed such a spectrum. So I thought, he doesn't bang his head against the wall and he has language—and that's all I really knew about autism.

My sister called me one day and said, "My friend's son was just diagnosed with Asperger's and he sounds a lot like Oliver." And I remember she prefaced the whole thing with, "I don't want to scare you." So I went on the Internet and read all about it. He certainly had some things; other things he didn't. I didn't believe it. And then I took out books and read. I remember being devastated for a week or two. Then we had to regroup and find a way, a path we could take.

Nathan: We knew it was Asperger's before the diagnosis. I think it came as a relief. Putting the name on it helps to a degree, and it helps other people to understand. It doesn't necessarily answer questions because they'll see a range of behaviors. It was a good beginning and a good way to talk to teachers and other people about what would help him.

Cathy: We put together a history of Oliver that connected it all and clearly showed he had Asperger's. When we finally got the diagnosis it was the beginning of the good stuff. You figure, if your son has autism or Asperger's that's when the devastation should start, but for us, that's when the solutions could start. I remember feeling like now I was his ally. We could work on

everything together, whereas before, I was banging my head against the wall, not understanding.

I thought the saddest stories were the kids who hadn't had a diagnosis until they were 18. It's hard to hear something about yourself for the first time when you're that age, or at any point in adolescence. I thought it's much better to grow up with the knowledge and feel comfortable with who you are.

Nathan: I wondered if we could magically give him all the support and help that he needed without telling him anything. Could this help him not to internalize problems or accept the diagnosis as a limitation? Oliver understood early that in many ways he was different. For one thing, he had a one-to-one aide in the classroom. Having an explanation for the difference is ultimately more helpful than feeling that you're different and not being sure about it. I think what we did was best for Oliver.

Cathy: He's a completely amazing kid. I tell him that if they ever found a cure for autism, I wouldn't want him to have it because he wouldn't be the same person. He sees the world in a different way. I think of him as a gift. He has so much love and he's so full of sweetness. So, all of the challenges that come along with it are so overshadowed by who he is. It's been way more positive than it has been negative. And at times it's been devastatingly negative. Oliver is wonderful. I wouldn't want him to be any different unless it would make him a happier person. He's a very happy kid.

One of the greatest gifts that we ever gave to Oliver was his sister Nora. They adore each other and she basically taught him how to play. Her interactions with him always made him feel very comfortable at home—because he wasn't with the rest of the world. One day he put his arms around her and said, "I love you," I couldn't believe it because he had never said that to me even though I knew he adored me. That was such a wonderful thing for him—he was always so good to her.

Nathan: Oliver is a goodhearted person. It hasn't seemed like an effort to be accepting of him. A diagnosis doesn't change the individual. Everyone is an individual; and there is a spectrum of people within a diagnosis and people outside the diagnosis. It's always about dealing with each other one on one.

Cathy: Oliver is doing beautifully, he's into adolescence and he's much taller than I am. Every single year we think about where Oliver is going to be. What's Oliver going to be like? You really have to take one day at a time. We've had lots of peaks and lots of valleys through the years, but we've always been optimistic.

suzanne
reyes

Suzanne Reyes and Bob Scheinerman have two children—
Calida, who has an autism spectrum disorder, and their
younger daughter, Olivia, whom they adopted from Korea.
Theirs is a wonderful family defined by love and acceptance
rather than by difference. Suzanne and Bob have many
important life lessons to share.

Calida is so special: every thing that she does, every word that she says, every hug that I get, is, in my mind, a miracle.

Calida is our first child. I wasn't around a lot of other little children when I was younger, so I had no experience with little children. When we first saw some of her social differences, because she was so young, it was easy for me and even for the doctors at that point to say, "Let's not worry about it yet. It's not that big a deal." But my husband, who had seen his nieces and nephews grow up around him, knew that something wasn't right: Calida wouldn't come to other people or want us to be a part of her play, and she wouldn't share her toys and didn't play like other kids typically did.

At a family gathering when she was about 16 months old, we asked my sister-in-law, who's a special ed teacher, to take a look at her and play with her. My husband and I went for a walk and let her play with our daughter. When we came back, my sister-in-law didn't say autism, but she did say, "You need to take her to a specialist. She's not doing some of the things she should be."

We took her to see a neurologist. At the age of 20 months, Calida was diagnosed with an autism spectrum disorder. When we went back and saw the doctor after the six months mark, she said, "We need to bump up the therapy; this isn't enough." She didn't see as many changes as she would like to have seen. We knew that this was it; this was something that we'd be changing our whole life for. The hardest thing to accept was that the whole future we had thought of for our daughter was gone. Everyone's got a future in their mind about what their child's going to do. At the point that you accept the diagnosis and know that it's true, that whole future is gone. You have to accept a new reality.

In order to accept it, we thought we had to do what was best for our daughter. We also were not going to accept that this is all she's going to be. I started researching everything I could about autism, all the various treatments and what could be done and how she can be helped. I made it my life to help Calida. We just

made a decision that we'll do everything we can for this child. We truly believe that over the years and in the long run, she will be okay. She might grow up to be a little quirky, but a very bright and successful adult in her own right. That's what we are continuing to shoot for with all the approaches we've taken with her and all the therapies that we've given her and all the medical treatments. And it's ongoing; it never ends.

I took the grief and the depression and decided that I just had to take action. That was my own therapy, my own personal therapy. I was going to do whatever I could. In some ways I feel this is what I was supposed to be. It's truly changed our lives, and I feel like a better person because of this. It's taught me a lot about life and what's important. It's also made me appreciate my child all that much more. She is so special. Every thing that she does, every word that she says, every hug that I get, is, in my mind, a miracle. You never take any progress for granted.

Calida has a little sister now. Her name is Olivia, and we adopted her from Korea when she was 12 months old. It was a long time coming. We waited many years before we decided to have another child; it was a question of whether to have a biological child or adopt. Initially, I was willing to take the risk and have another child, because I loved Calida so much. I thought, "I don't care, it doesn't matter if we end up with another child in the spectrum 'cause she's wonderful." My husband was a little more concerned. And I got diagnosed with some health issues—I was suspected of having lupus. The doctors were concerned enough to say that pregnancy could accelerate the disease and make my health worse. And so that was the deciding factor. So we adopted Olivia—Olivia and Calida really seem to love each other.

We continue to go through what a lot of parents call the roller coaster of emotions. As we work with our daughter and try to help her and make her better, we're optimistic about her outlook and how her progress is going. But then we see another child that's about the same age who is doing all the typical things that a child Calida's age would do. And you don't resent that child, but it's just a reminder of what your child's not doing. So then you're going on the down side of the roller coaster and feeling sad again. And then something else happens and you're back up. But then a family event comes around, and you can't participate in the same way as your cousins or whatever because your child can't tolerate noises and large crowds. We had to be very careful about what we did, and we missed a lot. Those situations would make us feel a little sad.

If I were talking to a parent of an autistic child who had just gotten the diagnosis, I would want them to know that they will find their place, and that they will find peace with it—in their own way. The most important thing for them is just to focus on their child and focus on their family and keep it strong and just love their child.

loyda
maldonado

Loyda and her husband, Augusto, adore their son Santiago. Although autism limits Santiago's ability to communicate verbally, the bonds of love that their family shares run deep and strong. They thank God for the progress that Santiago is making and for the simple pleasures that he is able to enjoy. To see Santiago happy means the world to them.

Parents have their hearts stolen by autism.

I told my husband the diagnosis, but he didn't believe it, because at that time, we had no idea about autism. But we read more about this problem, and somebody advised me to get some help at the regional center. They had classes Wednesday nights and Saturdays. For three years I went to different meetings held at the regional center. I learned a lot, and that helped me psychologically.

I tried to train my daughter, too. I brought her to the meetings at the regional center, and she learned a lot. I got a book about autism for her and she prepared a lot of work about autism for her presentation at the school. She got an A on that assignment. Sometimes it affected her, which is normal. But she continued in school, and she got married when she was 18 years old.

Santiago's doing great at school because since the beginning we've been teaching him sign language, and we began with the PECS system, too. I feel happy because he's thinking. He's really improving. He's getting better every day. I noticed the changes—he has his own personality. When he wants something, he lets me know by pointing at the item or by going and getting what he wants. I always try to be ready, to help him in everything. To see him happy is important for me. When we go someplace to eat, he tells me what he wants to eat. My dream is just that he tells me, "Mama, I want juice or I want to go out. I love you." That would be enough for me really, to hear that from my son.

Parents have their hearts stolen by autism. So it's good for the parents to be educated in the problem. If not, they cannot help. My advice: give a lot of love. Don't focus on the negative things. Find the positive things in your child. Put the attention to the positive thing, and that's the way to help your kids.

I say, "God, let us do everything we can with him." So that's why I'm so happy. I have a very great hope. I hope that God is helping me in everything. I wanted to have a special place for Santiago, and I got it. It's in Mexico, in Kilometer 96, Tecate, Mexicali. It's a little house, on a big piece of land. Santiago can see mountains and he loves the mountains. In the afternoon he loves to see the sunset and sits in a special place just watching the

sunset. And he loves to see the stars. So we vacation there frequently. He loves that place.

My husband helps me with Santiago. He likes to plant. He loves to garden. Santiago sometimes waters the plants with him, because he likes to do it, too. My husband hopes that God is going to help Santiago, through his therapies, with the help of technology advances, which are now in place. Those are some of my husband's hopes.

lalik
martin

It has been a long and difficult road for Lalik Martin and her son, Avi. When Avi was a child, Lalik often felt alone—just she and Avi to face all of the struggles that autism spectrum disorders can impose. Today, she feels that it was all worthwhile as they look to a more promising future for Avi.

I am so lucky to have Avi in my life...he gives me more than I give him.

In the very beginning, it was difficult for Avi and me because nobody understood us and there was no support system. I didn't know what was wrong and Avi's doctors didn't know either. And at that time, there was no support system, no-one. Avi's father couldn't handle it and left. My mother said that I was a bad mother because I didn't know how to discipline Avi, because of the things that Avi did. People told me that I was just not a good mother to Avi, that I spoiled him.

I knew that something was wrong, but nobody would listen to me. Avi did not talk, he wouldn't talk. He screamed, he always screamed. So they told me that he was spoiled again. He didn't want to eat food, so I had to get his favorite takeout every day to make sure that he ate something. And then I used feel like I was a hostage, because he was screaming so much.

When he went to kindergarten, his teacher told me that I had separation anxiety—and she was supposed to be a very good teacher. That didn't help, of course.

Finally one day when he was seven, I took Avi to the emergency room and I told the doctor, "I'm not taking him home because he's in danger." Avi was climbing on the second-story window, an open window with a broken screen. He would climb on stuff in the house and he was breaking stuff. He would have blackouts and he would put nails into the sockets. Avi just didn't know what he was doing. I stayed in emergency about four hours with Avi, and they brought all kinds of people to see him: psychiatrists, psychologists, physicians, everything, and they admitted him to a psychiatric hospital.

After five days in the hospital, his doctor told me he was autistic. And I said, "Autistic, this doesn't happen in my family," and I started to cry. The doctor told me Avi would never amount to anything. He said he would never be able to read and write. He said he would never go to school and graduate or do anything. I could not look forward to any kind of future for him.

Today Avi is nothing like what he used to be. Avi learned through his brother; Avi learned through his school; Avi learned

through everyone. It's not one person, it's not only me, it's the whole community, it's everybody. Avi learned how to be like a mensch. Avi is so polite, and he has developed a great sense of humor—he is wonderful. He knows exactly what he has. He accepts it. He wants to have a good job; he wants to get married; he wants to have children; he wants to be a business man. I think he'll be able to do whatever he sets his mind to.

I am so lucky that I have Avi in my life. He is a very special human being. I look up to him. Through his disability, Avi really came into my heart.

elly and john
schneider

Elly and John Schneider went the distance when they realized that their son Chasen had Asperger's Disorder. With love and commitment, Elly home-schooled Chasen for several years, and John became a celebrity parent spokesperson for children with autism spectrum disorders and their families. They are a constant source of encouragement to other parents.

What I want others to know is that they can do it.

John: The pediatrician noticed some unusual behavior with Chasen when he was two and a half. He said, "I think you need to have Chasen tested to see what's going on." Chasen was exhibiting echolalia, repetitive speech. He would say what we said over and over and over again. So he enjoyed the speaking, but he wasn't making any sense, he wasn't expressing himself.

Elly: Finally, one doctor told me that Chasen has an autism spectrum disorder, and I believe that labeling is extremely helpful for a parent—not to put their child in a box, but to be able to learn more. That's what helped me the most. I went out and found everything I could on autism, but something didn't sit right with me. I could understand why she would say that Chasen had some of those characteristics, but it just did not sit well with me. Over the next year, I acted as if he had autism. I didn't believe that he did, but I still treated him as such because I wanted to give him all the opportunities possible. I kept asking other parents of children who are going through the same thing, and they were a wealth of information. That's when I started reading about Asperger's, and I thought, "Okay, this is what it is."

John: Chasen responded well to speech and language therapy and went from there to occupational therapy. Chasen learns incredibly quickly. The notion that you have to hire an expert to teach your child to play is a little hard to come to grips with. Chasen went through a lot of that and now does really well. But some things that most children just kind of learn by osmosis need to be taught to a child with Asperger's.

Elly: Our son was asked to leave a private school when he was in third grade. It was very heartbreaking for us because he had done so well academically, and we wanted so much for him to continue being successful in school. Chasen had inappropriate social skills and couldn't behave properly. He couldn't sit in class.

Noise bothered him. There was so much stimulation that he could not function. The teacher called and said, "There's nothing I can teach him anyway, because he's so advanced."

I checked out all of the schools that other people had told me about, but Chasen's so high functioning that I couldn't find a fit for him. I have known women who have home-schooled their children, and I would always say, "Good for you! That's amazing! How awesome!" But I never thought that I would ever do it, or had the ability to do it; but he's my child and there weren't any other options. I thought he would do really well one on one, and so that is what I did. I didn't do it all by myself: I used a computer for online curriculum, I took him to a home-schooling history class, and we made a lot of field trips. That's what made the biggest change in Chasen, being home-schooled for two years in the third and fourth grades. It gave him a calm, safe place to be all day, where he didn't have to function for seven hours straight. When they asked Chasen to leave that school, I didn't want to leave Karis, our then ten-year-old daughter, there; so I home-schooled them both at the same time.

John: Karis is our tree climber, our soccer player, and our amazingly coordinated little girl. She was Chasen's social skills class 101—and 201. And I think that was very helpful. For fifth grade, Chasen went back to school. There are some challenges, but our doctor works with the teachers.

Elly: What I want others to know is that they can do it. You can do anything you put your minds to. Everything we've had to learn to do with Chasen, we've had to learn ourselves. As long as you're willing, I don't think there's anything that anyone can't do.

John: If there's an opportunity to get on a platform and speak to people who are going through the beginnings of this, or whatever level or stage that they're going through, we want to support that. We want to let them know that it is hard; it's going take a lot of work. But there'll be tremendous benefits as a result. We've all changed by virtue of the work we that we've done. I don't think that it's something to hide; I think it is something to bring forth, to put in front of other people and say, "This is going to be difficult, but it's well worth the work."

peggy and james
spalding

Jim Spalding and his wife Peggy decided to give Peggy's grandson, Corde, a chance at a better life when they adopted him at two and a half years of age. It was a kind and selfless act. Little did they suspect Corde's difficult beginnings would be compounded by an autism spectrum disorder. The Spaldings have selflessly given their love and support throughout the years.

We have the pleasure of knowing that what we're doing is important.

Peggy: Our grandson, Corde, has been with us since he was two and a half years old. His mother was mentally ill and a drug addict. So she's had her problems too, and to take care of them both was just too much. She was homeless at the time, and she wouldn't stay with us or my mother or her father. She took off with the baby. So here she has a new baby, going from homeless shelter to homeless shelter.

Jim: One day the judge finally gave custody of Corde to us because his mother didn't show up in court. It's not very often that adults get a second chance at raising children. When you've raised children, you can look back 20 or 30 years and think maybe you should have done or said things differently. And it's sort of nice to get a second chance to make up for the goofs that you made with the first three kids. We're retired folks, and maybe we're not enjoying our retirement as much as we should or can, but at the same time, it's a pleasure to be able to give something that you won't be able to give for very much longer. And I think this is an honor in a way; so that's how I look at it, simple as that. I was adopted; I was in an orphanage until I was 12 or 13. So this gives me a chance to give back as I was given to.

Once you get a diagnosis, then you know where to go for help. Everybody's always afraid: "Oh, don't call my child mentally disturbed or autistic or anything because it'll stigmatize them." But you need a label to get some help. So the first thing is to get somebody to evaluate and see what's wrong.

Peggy: Just keep plugging away; that's about all you can do. Well, I guess I'm fortunate that I married Jim, because my ex-husband probably wouldn't have gone along with this. Jim's mother adopted three children, two girls and a boy. She always said, "Well, I invest in children, not in the stock market." So that's probably where he got this drilled into him, that you should invest in children.

Jim: During the last year, Corde said he knows why I want him to read: "You're worried about me. You want me to be successful. I know that, Grandpa." I replied, "You're right, that's why. Because no one in society is going to give a darn about whether you're successful or not; you're just one more number. But to yourself you're important, and to us you're important. So you will become successful because of you. You'll become successful because that's what you want to be. And to get an education, to learn to read and write, is one more step of being successful."

You keep thinking, "When I retire, I'm going to do this, I'm going to do that, I'm going to travel, I'm going to buy this and going to buy that." We're retired, and we really don't have time to do all those things that are supposedly so great. But, you know, we do have the pleasure of knowing that what we're doing is important. And we are getting pleasure in doing it. So that's what we get out of it, and I think that's enough.

major general doron
almog

Doron Almog is a retired Israeli general who served his country for 35 years. He and his brother Eran fought in the Yom Kippur war. His brother did not survive. Doron would find out that his brother was still alive when he was left behind. At that moment, Doron made a vow never to leave a soldier behind. When his son was born, he named him Eran in memory of his brother. When Eran was diagnosed with autism, Doron vowed never to leave a child with special needs behind and to help provide for their futures as adults. Through his efforts, a 25-acre residential community in Israel recently opened its doors—it is called Aleh Negev.

...these kids can be hostages for all of their lives.

The first crisis of parents is about broken expectations. It's unbelievable what a crisis it is to be a father and a mother of a child with autism. We started speaking about the meaning of life, why were we punished. What have we done? What's wrong? We came to the same conclusion—we'll love Eran. We'll never be ashamed. We'll speak about him among our friends. We'll teach our daughter, Nitzan, to love him.

Eran will never have the power to fight for himself, to speak for himself, to manipulate, or to lobby. I don't know what he knows. So I'm always asking myself what I should do for him, and I'm always thinking about how he is feeling and whether he is happy. And it was through sensing him, looking into his eyes and trying to understand his nature, and trying to understand his satisfaction, his happiness, and his joy.

Some children with autism have no ability to understand, or maybe we don't have the ability to understand them. It seems to me sometimes that we don't know the code, how to break the code, how to understand them. They know a different language. It's not English. It's not Hebrew. It's not French. It's not Russian. It's a different language we must try to learn to get to their soul, their psyche, and to bring them to maximum capacity.

My wife, Didi, and I look at Eran and he's smiling. To bring a smile to Eran's face, only a smile, is one of our goals. We learned it's not about our broken expectations, it's about him.

When he was 17, I decided to fight publicly about the issue of the weakest in our society because most parents are ashamed when their son or daughter has a severe disability like Eran. They are ashamed that they will never be normal, won't continue the legacy of the family and won't get married and bear children. I vowed to leave no soldier behind after my brother Eran died in the Yom Kippur War in October, 1973. I was the first Israeli soldier to land in Entebbe in the famous daring rescue operation on July 4, 1976. The hostages of Entebbe were kept for one week; these children can be hostages for all of their lives. My brother is gone; my son is alive, fully dependent on my power, my health and my commitment.

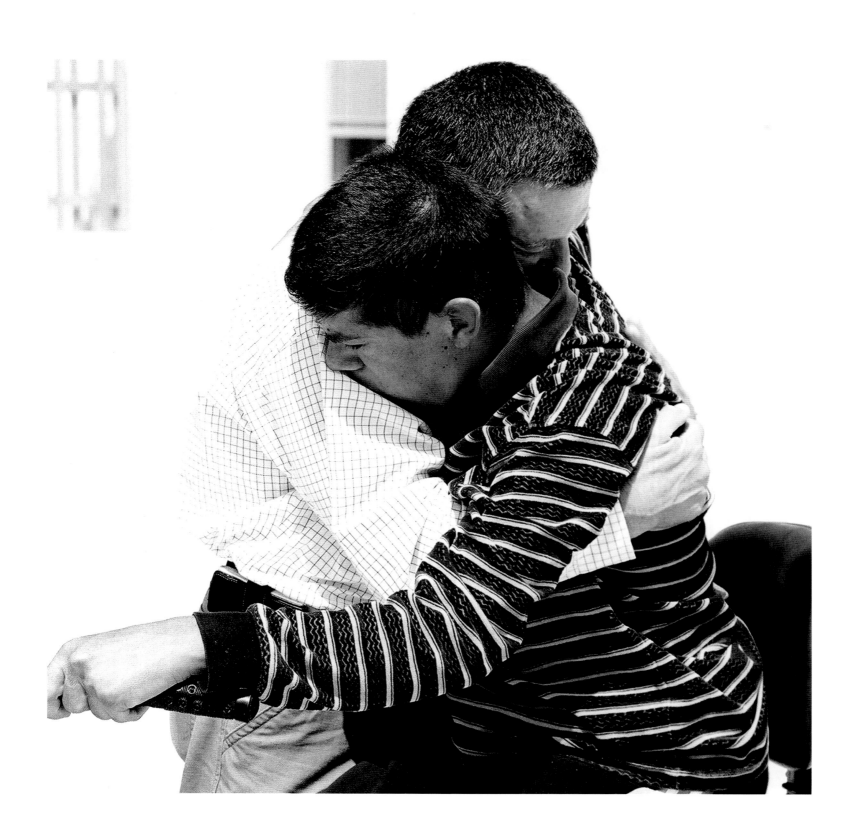

Eran gives me a lot of power: to walk for him, to be his mouthpiece, to fight for him, to guarantee his future, because I won't live forever, to change public attitudes and to give power to many parents.

I decided to build a village in Israel called Aleh Negev for seriously disabled children when they become adults. It is for young people like Eran who have a combination of retardation and autism and physical limitations. We are building a future for them. Aleh opened recently, and my son lives there in an environment that is accepting, therapeutic and supportive.

He is now a young adult and has never said one word, not even "Dad." Yet Eran is the most meaningful person in my life. He taught me so much about myself. He's the greatest professor of my life. He's the one who made me so sensitive to human life.

■   ■   ■

Since the interview, Doron's beloved son Eran passed away due to medical illness. Doron continues his important work in honor of his son's memory. After Eran's passing, the village's name was changed to Aleh Negev-Nachalat Eran.

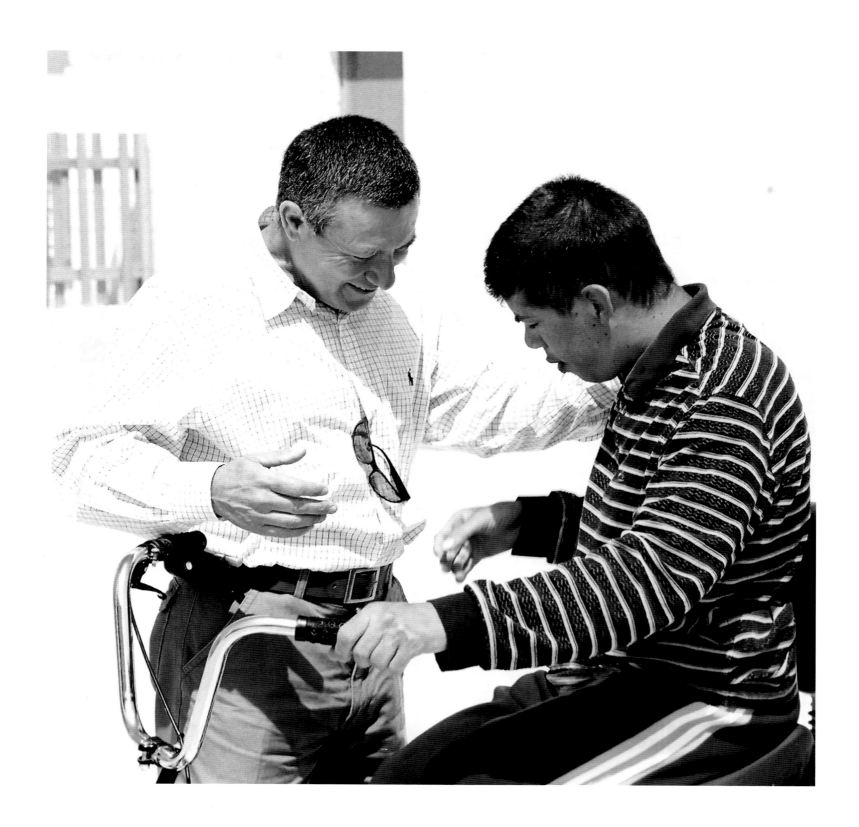

levisa
wade

L
ike all parents, the Wades had wonderful dreams for their
son Darnell's future—dreams they had to redefine given
the magnitude of Darnell's disability. Although Darnell
has autism and is non-verbal, there is a beautiful discourse of
love and affection between him and his parents that takes place
each and every day.

For parents, it's a very different lifelong commitment.

When I hear people tell me that their child is autistic, my heart goes out to them. As I look back at the road that I've been down, it wasn't easy, especially since Darnell was my first child. I still get overwhelmed thinking about it. I want to share all the knowledge and experience we have inside us to help other people.

Last year was the first time I ever went to a parent support group and I really wish I had done it much sooner. I had a very good support group with my friends and my family. But they don't understand the day-in and the day-out of having a child with autism. They can sympathize with you but they can't understand you like another parent who has an autistic child. Last year the support group helped me to understand that I had done everything there was to do for Darnell.

I see myself as an advocate for my child. I have to go out and fight for my child. We've done everything to get him to the place he's at today and it's so rewarding that now we can help other people.

When I take Darnell into the community I would like the public to know that these children don't misbehave because they want to. You have to look through their eyes and imagine what they are going through—it's not something that they want to go through and if you have questions, instead of just staring at the child or the parent just ask. Lately, people have been more understanding and it makes me feel really good. I'll even have people come over to me when they see that Darnell is having a hard time and pat me on the shoulder and say it's going to be okay.

I think that Darnell has brought my husband and me closer. My husband came with me to group settings with Darnell and other children whereas a lot of fathers stayed away. One of Darnell's therapists asked us if we ever had any type of marital problems that would tear us apart due to Darnell's autism. We looked at each other and said no.

I think that men have trouble with things that they can't control or can't fix, especially since my husband is a fire captain. He's always there to fix things and this is something he couldn't fix. But instead of shying away, he got closer.

In thinking about the future, I hope that Darnell will be functional at a level where he can take care of himself to some degree, at least to a point where others won't take advantage of him. For parents in our situation, it's a very different lifelong commitment. My husband and I have already planned for him to be with us for the rest of our lives.

You have to come to the realization that some things aren't going to happen. Darnell doesn't have to talk, as long as he can communicate in a way to let us know what he wants.

For the longest time I always used to ask my husband, "Do you think he knows who I am? Does he know I'm his Mom?" Now, I do know that he does.

afterword

So much has changed during the years I have been involved in helping children with special needs. The momentum in the field of autism has never been greater than it is today.

Science moves forward in both basic and applied research, greater focus is being placed on the use of best practices that are built on evidence-based recommendations in assessment and intervention, and advocacy groups continue to promote positive change. Public policies are being examined and reshaped to address the compelling need for services. The ongoing controversies and the quest for definitive answers stimulate important dialogue and debate. With the exposure of the issues of autism by the mainstream media and other public awareness efforts, the public is becoming better informed and eager for change.

Currently, I am serving as Vice-chair of the California Legislative Blue Ribbon Commission on Autism. This dynamic initiative is charged with the responsibility of identifying gaps in service for individuals with autism across the lifespan and to make recommendations to the governor and legislature regarding the closing of these gaps. After a recent public hearing, parents said that they had never been more encouraged and now felt that real change was in the making—rather than just another report to gather dust on a shelf. Proactive processes like this one are taking place around the world, signaling hope to families everywhere.

Nevermore "the monster in the closet," or the "Scarlet Letter," the stigma of autism is in the process of being fully and forever lifted by the light of greater understanding and acceptance. Society is becoming more fully engaged in the agenda of ensuring brighter futures for all children with autism spectrum disorders.

The forces for change are palpable and unstoppable. The heart and soul of all of these efforts to create this new horizon of hope is the worldwide community of autism heroes—families meeting the challenge.

selected reading for families

This reading list is meant to provide a broad range of information for families who are beginning to confront the challenges of autism spectrum disorders.

Attwood, T. (2005) *The Complete Guide to Asperger's Syndrome*. London: Jessica Kingsley Publishers.

Bashe, P.R. and Kirby, B.L. (2005) *The OASIS Guide to Asperger Syndrome: Completely Revised and Updated: Advice, Support, Insight and Inspiration*. New York: Crown Publishers.

Exkorn, K.S. (2005) *The Autism Sourcebook: Everything You Need to Know About Diagnosis, Treatment, Coping and Healing*. New York: Regan Books.

Grandin, T. (1995) *Thinking in Pictures and Other Reports from My Life with Autism*. New York: Doubleday Publishers.

Klass, P. and Costello, E. (2003) *Quirky Kids*. New York: Ballantine Books.

Lord, C. and McGee, J. (2001) *Educating Children with Autism*. Washington, D.C.: National Academy Press.

Ozonoff, S., Dawson, G. and McPartland, J. (2002) *A Parent's Guide to Asperger Disorder and High-Functioning Autism: How to Meet the Challenges and Help Your Child Thrive*. New York: The Guilford Press.

Powers, M.D. (2000) *Children with Autism: A Parent's Guide*. Second edition. Baltimore, MD: Woodbine Publishers.

Schreibman, L. (2005) *The Science and Fiction of Autism*. Massachusetts: Harvard University Press.

Willey, L. H. (1999) *Pretending to be Normal: Living with Asperger's Syndrome*. London: Jessica Kingsley Publishers.

Wing, L. (2001) *The Autistic Spectrum: A Parent's Guide to Understanding and Helping Your Child*. Berkeley, CA: Ulysses Press.

Wiseman, N. (2006) *Could It Be Autism? A Parent's Guide to the First Signs and Next Steps*. New York: Broadway.

about the help group

The Help Group — because every child deserves a great future

Founded in 1975, The Help Group is the largest, most innovative and comprehensive nonprofit organization of its kind in the United States serving children with special needs related to autism, Asperger's Disorder, learning disabilities, ADHD, mental retardation, abuse and emotional problems.

The Help Group's six specialized day schools offer pre-K through high school programs for more than 1,300 students. The Help Group's wide range of mental health and therapy services, child abuse and residential programs extend its reach to more than 5,000 children and their families each year. With over 800 staff members, its state-of-the-art schools and programs are located on four major campuses in the Los Angeles area.

The Help Group is highly regarded for its high standards of excellence and unique scope and breadth of services. Through its public awareness, professional training and parent education programs and efforts at the state and national levels, The Help Group touches the lives of children with special needs across the country and in other parts of the world.

At the heart of its effort is the commitment to helping young people fulfill their potential to lead positive, productive and rewarding lives.

The Help Group's Autism Schools and Programs

Recognized as a leader in the field of autism, The Help Group offers extensive special education, treatment and therapy services. The Help Group educates over 750 students ages three to 22 in its innovative autism day schools on a daily basis. It offers diagnostic assessments, intervention, family support, after-school social skills groups and summer day camps. In addition extensive outreach and parent and professional training opportunities are offered.

The Help Group Center for Autism Spectrum Disorders

The Help Group Center for Autism Spectrum Disorders is an outpatient program serving children 12 months to 18 years of age. The center provides diagnostic evaluations using the latest research-based assessment tools and offers state-of-the-art developmental, psycho-educational and neuro-psychological assessments, as well as individual, family and group therapy.

Young Learners Preschool for Autism is a highly specialized and intensive education and early intervention day school designed to serve children between three and five years of age with autism spectrum disorders, including classical autism, high-functioning autism, Asperger's Disorder and Pervasive Developmental Disorder—Not Otherwise Specified (PDD-NOS). This unique day school offers an intensive six hours per day, special education program with all support services incorporated into the school day.

Village Glen School is a multidisciplinary therapeutic day school with an emphasis on social skills training for students with Asperger's Disorder, high-functioning autism, anxiety-related disorders and non-verbal learning disabilities. Village

Glen's Pace Program is available for gifted students and its Beacon Program is designed for students with accompanying behavioral challenges. Village Glen also offers a summer day camp designed to facilitate social skills development in a highly structured, fun and supportive environment.

Bridgeport School educates students ages five to 22 and integrates an academic curriculum with hands on, life skills training and vocational services. Its program is designed for students with mild cognitive delays and challenges with social communication and/or language development, many of whom have autism spectrum disorders.

Sunrise School for Autism & Developmental Disabilities is a special education day school for students, ages five to 22, with moderate global delays associated with autism and other developmental disabilities. Its curriculum promotes communicative, behavioral, social, academic, motor, adaptive and independent living skills.

Pacific Schools address the needs of students who require an intensive therapeutic day school due to emotional and behavioral disabilities. Its Pacific Cove Program is designed for students with social communication disabilities, including high-functioning autism and Asperger's Disorder who have significant behavioral challenges.

Project Six: Developmental Disabilities Program provides therapeutic living opportunities in nurturing, home-like settings for young adults and adults with developmental disabilities, including autism.

The Help Group National Autism Foundation

The Help Group National Autism Foundation was established in 2005 to promote greater awareness, early identification, early intervention, education and treatment opportunities for children, adolescents and young adults with autism spectrum disorders (ASDs). The foundation provides educational seminars, conferences, and publications for professionals and parents, and promotes outreach efforts in underserved communities.

The Help Group—UCLA Autism Research Alliance

The Help Group—UCLA Autism Research Alliance is an innovative partnership between The Help Group and the UCLA Semel Institute for Neuroscience and Human Behavior. It is dedicated to enhancing and expanding clinical research in ASD education and treatment and to contributing to the development, greater understanding and use of best practice models by educators and clinicians.

ASD Parent Support Network

The Help Group's ASD Parent Support Network offers ongoing support groups designed for parents and families of children and adolescents with autism spectrum disorders. This network provides a caring environment for parents to share experiences, network, and learn coping and intervention strategies from other parents as well as professionals.

www.thehelpgroup.org